THE GREAT BRITISH WRITE OFF

IMMERSED IN WORDS

Edited by Jenni Bannister

forwardpoetry

First published in Great Britain in 2014 by:
Forward Poetry
Remus House
Coltsfoot Drive
Peterborough
PE2 9BF

Telephone: 01733 890099
Website: www.forwardpoetry.co.uk

Book Design by Ali Smith

SB ISBN 978-1-84418-686-0

Printed and bound in the UK by BookPrintingUK
Website: www.bookprintinguk.com

Foreword

Here at Forward Poetry our aim has always been to provide a bridge to publication for unknown poets and allow their work to reach a wider audience. We believe that poetry should not be exclusive or elitist but available to be accessed and appreciated by all.

Our latest competition **'The Great British Write Off'** was created to celebrate the writing talent we have here in the UK. We invited poets and authors to write either a poem, a short story or even an extract from a novel that showcases their ability. The result is an entertaining collection of creative writing that expresses and communicates thoughts, feelings and ideas on a multitude of subjects. A panel of judges will now choose their top 3 authors, who will win either the first prize of £1450.50, the second prize of a Book Printing voucher worth £500 or the third prize of £100.

Whether you prefer humorous rhymes, poignant odes or a thrilling short story, there is something in these pages to suit every reader's taste. We are very proud to present this anthology and we are sure it will provide entertainment and inspiration for years to come.

Contents

The Creative Writing

Veni, Vidi, Vici

Life was lived here, once;
love, loved and lost,
war and work discussed.
Air was breathed and halls were walked,
and men and women had their being.

What a privilege
to stand where you once stood
and see the walls and floors of your dominion.
To breathe the past like air
and picture every moment of your life
as if a single day had not passed by
and you would tread these hallways still.

But like snow in spring,
your presence is long gone.
All that remains is a memory,
a footprint,
a ***whisper***
of all that you once were.

As I walk your broken floors,
I almost feel you beside me
And across the span of years
I hear you say
'We have conquered even time.'

Rebecca Campling

No One Lives Here Anymore

Viewed, as it were, from in the lane the building looks largely the same
Though close inspection shows neglect and what a stranger might expect
Who couldn't care just what he'd seen and had no feel for what had been
For this once was a vibrant home with memories so dear to some
Inside invites a sad despair, a broken toy, a crooked chair
With faded carpets down the halls, exhausted paintings on the walls
Trapped sunshine there that none will see and dust motes writhing endlessly
A house that once was full of life with happiness and sometimes strife
A sanctuary, sure and warm, and refuge from the raging storm
Compelling smells of new-baked bread and cosy feelings safe in bed
Great muddy boots on polished floors and sticky fingers on the doors
Lost echoes to the longing ear that spent a happy childhood here
Unbridled laughter on the stairs and shoes that never came in pairs
When Christmases had lights so bright, excitement on that magic night
Those summer mornings, long hot days and later hills all lost in haze
The nectar-drunken bees outside would sense the breeze and catch a ride
And ancient cobwebs still trap prey, the hunter long has gone away
A last look back then close the door, for no one lives here anymore

Michael Rodgerson

Are We In This Together?

Knowing that you are attached to a materialistic paper fallacy in life,
Makes feeding the need for that paper fallacy a struggling toll each and every single day.
Chained and shackled,
Breadline of society,
Finding it a struggle,
We ought to know it's not right.
What happened to love thy neighbour?
Not judging a book by its cover?
It seems all you do,
Is cast scorn on the meek.
Identifying them by a faceless number,
No personality of to speak,
Cast out into the cold,
If they do not follow the marching of your beat.

Michael Harkins

Disbelief

Even when it stopped raining
they didn't.
They couldn't.
What did you expect? it said,
she said, he said.
It said, she said, he said.
Lightning bolts and well
we don't quite know,
But not you.
Not you, they said.
And the locusts didn't
Come so how could they?
Is it enough that I am
What I am? it said,
she said, he said.
It said, she said, he said.
But you gotta prove it,
With a miracle or some such,
they said.
They said.
It sighed, she sighed, he sighed.
It sighed, she sighed, he sighed,
And clicked the fingers of the
Right hand. Not again.
They destroyed everything; they were gone.

Jack Desambrois

Stirrer In A Stew

The Wooden Spoon is a treasured utensil,
Just as important as a poet's Pencil.
It's like Ireland's most precious Holy Grail,
It will end up pleasing you, without fail.
What it conjures up will blow your mind,
Your needs will be fulfilled, you will find.
The end result will taste no less than first class,
Warms you up on cold nights, after church or Mass.
But it is only magical used with other things,
A giant pot and ingredients and a cooker ring.
My wee Granny would stir it vigorously all in a mix,
While Granda stocked the fire with broken sticks.
First Granny would brown all of the meat,
With all of the grandkids around her feet.
Then added the freshly peeled spuds and all of the veg,
While Granda cut Nutty Krust as thick as a window ledge.
This is a whole collage of flavours, aromas and taste,
Fills you up inside and outside and enlarges your waist.
They say it's best leaving it and eating it on the second day,
Even though you're hovering over it like it is your prey.
Taking a sneaky spoonful of it when nobody's around,
As you sniff out the meaty scent, like you are a hound.
Nothing beats it with a heal of a loaf and loads of butter,
With a mouthful of this, you won't be able to talk or utter.
Yes it is our tongue-tantalising bowl of hearty Irish stew,
The best meal in the world, take our word for it, it's true.
Our Irish stew washed down with our traditional stout,
Now that's what we call food and drink, without a doubt.

Gregory Mcilwaine

Hope In The Darkness

The trees sway in the breeze to a silent tune of misery as she stands in the pouring rain, tears streaming down her face. She's been here before in this lonely hell, this dark bottomless pit of despair. The candle which once burned bright had been blown out long ago, the hope disappeared out of her grasp, her soul blackened by the demons hiding inside, her heart broken into a million of pieces and her trust in everything... destroyed.
She feels so alone, so unloved and desperate, the scars which line her arms remind her of the past, the present and most certainly her future; so she stands watching the world go by knowing she's an outsider, knowing she'll never fit in, but to her that's alright, she wants to go unnoticed, she's living in her own world and it's safe and comfortable here. She's wary and guarded but yet she feels like letting you in, only you, for she already trusts you. Those nights of tossing and turning plagued with bad dreams, memories of the past, of that day which claimed her innocence; she knows in a flash you would make it all disappear, you'd replace her dark world with one filled with light and love. She would be happy to spend eternity in your arms, being held, being safe.
She'd spend forever loving you.

Rachel Lendrum

There Was A Morning That I Woke

There was a morning that I woke
And thought,
I might not have that long
To labour on as usual
To right all things done wrong
I realised, this precious life
Should never be in vain
Each one of us has got a gift
To make this life more sane
Dig deep and think what you can find
And make the world around more kind

Ursula Chaplin

Olympus Is Falling

One hundred tonnes of water plunges off the edge of a magnificent waterfall and crashes to the bottom where the vapours and steam rise from the permanently disturbed pool.
A tributary meanders off into the lush green valley, where the sounds of exotic animals echo through the trees, and the dew on every leaf sparkles like stars. The river then flows out into the vast open sea, giving a panoramic view of nothing but the water meeting the clear blue sky, and the gentle ripples travelling along the silken surface.
Suddenly, with an ear-splitting screech, a fiery meteor plummets down from the heavens and crashes violently into the water, turning the sea to a deep shade of black and setting off an angry water cyclone through its depths. Lightning flashes. Thunder roars. Olympus itself seems to be falling from its heights. Humungous ice balls rage down in a flurry of chaos, disintegrating on contact with the scorching sea. All the while, it feels as though the world is being turned inside out and that Armageddon is upon us.
... With the TV remote in one hand, and a good ol' cuppa in the other, I can't help but wonder why we Brits always have to overdramatise a simple tea advertisement and waste good air time. For goodness sake, I could be watching my favourite episode of Tom and Jerry right now.

Naziyah Mahmood

Sandwiches

Little Jim's done something very bad!
He played a trick on his Mum and Dad,
and enjoyed an extra seaside tea –
wolfing down th' the fillings with some glee.
It would not been as bad, before
if bread had not met seaside floor.
And so, the butties, once so grand
have fillings that are mainly sand.
To avoid detection, he will sit
by the sandwiches, now full of grit.
Whilst Mum and Dad wonders, what's hiding in their tea?
That extra filling that's come from th' sea

Brian Francis Kirkham

Hope

Freedom, since I have never known you,
I am not sure what I am looking for.
Sunshine, I have heard of your brilliance and warmth
But my cold heart has never felt your touch
Colour, so vibrant and beautiful, tales I have been told
But I don't know what that means
Dreams, all I know is darkness and horror
Angels, bright and majestic
Will you free me from this prison?
This place that has ever felt foreign
Though I have spent my whole life in its embrace
This cold diamond has never been my mother
Though the only existence I have known,
Its solace has never reached my heart
I know there is so much out there,
Another existence perhaps
Life, life I have never lived
I want to live life, I want to see the light, feel the warmth
Experience love, joy, laughter, happiness
Won't you be my release? Won't you take me away?
Won't you be my hero?
Won't you fight for freedom and equity?
Won't you take me home?
For this existence is not my home.

Debra Ayis

The Future Maker – An Extract

He was the Future Maker. For whatever price you were willing to pay, he would construct a Future of precise possibilities. A stainless steel and crystal Future for the ambitious, a summer blue lake of tears for the melancholy, or a simple, smooth-textured Future of tranquillity.

He worked alone at the top of a modest hill and wove his Futures from what he observed. He dissected desires, unfolded dreams and moulded them with inspiration into the fabric of time itself. Few were ever disappointed with his work, for the result gave inevitability to the course of their lives, but an inevitability which was emotionally perfect, tuned to the individual's own dream world and not to the grossness of material life.

He was the Future Maker, but had despair as his constant companion and ambition his greatest tormentor. No matter how gifted he was or how skilled he had become, there was one Future that evaded him. He was unable to devise the joy of love – neither for himself or another. He had employed affection and friendship as part of his grander themes, and once had constructed a Future of unrepentant lust for one of his more undiscerning clients. Yet even that emotion had left him unfulfilled.

He would spend long hours seated outside his home, gazing across the grassy slopes beneath him. Ceaselessly, he would try to grasp the fleeting touch of lovers, the open smiles and the soft whispers, but always the true essence of the emotion eluded him. He himself had never experienced the brush of cool lips or the warmth of a gentle breath upon his cheek. His pleasures had always been cerebral. To him, his work was the ultimate expression of the mind. Observation and analysis were surely two of the greatest pleasures. Yet, he wondered and despaired.

Johnnie Atherton

A Lesson

The moon is low,
casually drifting toward earth,
time taken, peacefully reaching the end.
Beyond the pines, he glimmers,
politely through
a small beam beneath
the flickers over head.
He does not fear an end,
neither does he complain,
Only lingers, quietly.
Until he plays his part in the day
(casting shadows across the land)
until tomorrow, as once again
the universe calls upon him.

Anna Clifford

The Shadow

When out of the drawer the photograph fell,
It caught me off guard when I saw the look,
And smile on the face I knew so well,
In far gone days when the photo I took.
The stab of regret was all the more keen,
For I thought I had long got over the stage,
Of wishing and yearning for what might have been.
I took this snap when still of an age
To do things on impulse, without any thought
Of checking to see if the angle was right,
So there, on the photo, my shadow was caught
Reaching to touch her in the evening's long light.
Did the bond that once joined us need sunlight to stay?
For when passion's fire faded – it vanished away.

Tom Robertson

Old Before My Time

My bones are creaking
I ache in pain,
And yearly eye check-ups
Mean corrections again.

Wrinkled skin and laughter lines
I question what was so funny?
The older I get, the less I have
Swagger that is, not money.

Seeing teenagers misbehaving now
I only have one thing to say,
I tut my teeth and roll my eyes
It wouldn't have happened in my day!

I came in when the streetlights came on
I was in bed before it was night,
I had table manners, respect for my elders
I was raised just right.

Shops were closed on a Sunday
And what was a Happy Meal?
I loved a good ol' toad in the hole
It created a homely feel.

Schools had daily assemblies
And names on pegs for coats,
We had Rainbow and Noddy
5 channels and no remote.

We had cartons of milk at school
And in a 10p mix we got ten,
I'm adult, I'm grown up, I'm twenty-five
But how nicer life was back then.

I'm more mature that my age suggests
I'm old before my time,
I prefer music from the 60s to 80s
To the noise of 2009.

Tracey Robertson

Novel Extract: Soul Juice

I tasted blood. The taste was unmistakable: sharp and strong – all bitter and metallic. I wanted to spit the taste out of my mouth. I wiped a hand across my lips. Automatically I looked at my hand. Then I saw it. That scarlet liquid that was a little too watery. It had smeared down the length of the front of my index finger. Droplets of the glistening red fluid ran down to the fingernail. Then dripped, falling to explode on the surface of my Clarks shoes. The shoes were black but streaked with brown-grey mud; and now pocked with red splashes decorating the surface.

I had always hated the sight of blood; especially my own. The unsettling red liquid screamed out at me; setting my nerves on full alert. Alarm bells rang loud inside of my head, my stomach heaved unhappily and my vision trembled and started to blur. I could feel my legs weakening; small tremors going off at the knees.

'Don't be such a baby!' Danny Raeder said.

'You split my lip!' I said.

'I'll do worse if you don't stop blubbing.'

I looked up. I saw Danny's face through watering eyes. It was a distorted mask of callousness. His mouth was pulled hard to one side in a sneer revealing his yellow nicotine stained teeth. Not a pleasant sight.

'What did you do that for?' I said. The words seemed to shake as I pushed them out of my mouth.

'Just because,' he said, 'I can!'

Tony Northover

Jennie Cooper Saves The Universe

The rain grinds on into evening in the same unyielding way it had submerged the day. The constant drum-roll of drops blended with the distortion of the wind, masks the noise of two drunken girls as they stumble up an unlit side-street to pee in peace.

They head for home; an elongated journey due to the crab-like motion derived from drink. Finally crashing through the door to the flat; words of anger greet them from a bedroom at the end of the hall. Ignored, it subsides and drifts back to sleep. In a room that clearly stands as a shrine to dust and poor hygiene, clumsy movements extract a slab of vinyl and place it in a parody of carefulness on a record player of obvious vintage and developing nation origin. The fireside crackle gives way to the music which fills the hearts and heads of those bodies fatigued by club-land and downers.

Sleep is ushered in.

Dream

Morning is vicious, and so avoided. But hunger, hangovers and full bladders will force them to consciousness by afternoon.

They head to the bathroom for a purging of the system followed by a cleansing of the skin. Condensation forms on the outside of the cold tiles; droplets coalesce and descend down the white enamel, into the steaming bath; recycled in evaporation. The sweet face of Jennie breaks the surface of the water.

'The f**k's that smell?' Atop the white lavatory sits Karen, stoically awaiting the end of the runs.

Damian Docherty

The Lost Student

I stare helplessly at the passing buildings,
willing them to slow us down, to intervene, to press pause
But the city landscape moves unceasingly,
Each passing mile a stark reminder – a realisation
People tumble out of clubs, couples cling to each other, fighting the harsh Edinburgh breeze,
And I realise, that will never be me.
A young girl, her eyes full of promise is seated opposite me,
'Going to view the University' she proclaims to a calling friend.
I cannot help but feel a torment of sorrow,
There is no promise in my tomorrow.
'Next stop Waverly' the autocom reminds me.
The words surprise me, panic me.
'Only three more minutes' it says,
Three more minutes and then I too will join the cool Edinburgh breeze.
But I will not be clinging to anyone, or tumbling out of a club,
But out of the airport bus, my only companion a holdall bursting with law books.
The zip moans against the pressure of the books,
That load is much too heavy for such a small case to carry
Yet there is little that can be done to rectify the situation,
For those books are needed – after all, the case is only a case.
'Where to?' a thick Edinburgh accent demands as I step into a black taxi, interrupting my musings.
'Pollock Halls of Residence,' I mutter, failing to hide my tone of regret.
Without a word more, he begins the ascent towards Arthur's Seat,
Climbing, climbing, climbing.
And there it is in all its glory, 'Pollock Halls of Residence',
Or 'Pollock Halls of Sorrow'
And down I trudge to Basement, Room Six.
The nearby thud of music and laughter and sickly aroma of beer and pizza remind me I am back . . .
My heart, it fills with sorrow.
I clamber into my little bed, full of pressing fears.
Should I be back here?
I have no answer,
But my Good Shepherd, he's searching for his lost sheep
And so with mirth I sing aloud,
'What a friend I have in Jesus,

All my sins and grieves to bear,
What a privilege to carry,
Everything to God in prayer,
O what peace we often forfeit,
O what needless pain we bear,
All because we do not carry,
Everything to God in prayer'.

Clare Stevenson

Life Is Art

What's so 'fine' about art?
I see nothing 'fine' about Da Vinci or Shakespeare.
Who decides how ambitious our art can be?
Is it locked up, forgotten about and rend the only key?

Yes, my art has no utility –
but take from this what you will.
To consider art 'fine' is like calling the sun too bright,
taking all the stars from the sky and leaving it just night.

In the end, 'fine' is just a word but words are more than fine
and to underestimate what your words can do is like turning off a light,
filling it with indistinct silhouettes of a darker shade of white.

So look after your similes, adjectives and nouns,
be sure to spread them across a page and paint what's in your heart
then step back, contemplate and realise it's not art.

It's life.

Dominic Hartley

The Land Once Lost

There once was a breeze, in a
Land once lost
Which tickled the trees and the leaves, it tossed
Which danced on the water of the rivers of blue
And weaved through the branches of the Old Bamboo.
It swept through the hair of the passing people
It wrapped round the houses, the church and the steeple
It tied up the town in a ribbon of chills
It rolled and it tumbled down the sticky, muddy hills.
It tapped on the windows of cottages quaint
And it creaked the old doors with their cracked, faded paint
It rushed around full of glee, little sprite
Fun, free and frolic in the day, in the night.
Gentle in the summer, yet blind when cold
Come hither little breeze from a
Land so old.

Steffi McIntyre

Swimming

We went swimming that day, with the clear azure water, lapping the ceramic shore. And the three tone beep, to show, the waves were coming. The archway pool... morphed to an archway in the ocean, reminiscent of Durdledoor. Our feet padded, the watered floor, our own sea shore and I couldn't go on anymore. My legs found your hips, and my breasts pressed your back. Humans are so light in water, yet even with your tangerine peeling hands on my thighs, telling me I was grounded, I floated up. Soared in spirit. My neck dropped down, my head weighted, in the dip of your shoulder, to place a kiss on the cheek that was damp from splashes. Those awe-filled brown eyes, slid up in their pools of white, locked with mine and as one, we turned and gazed out, as the white wall changed to a sunset in the deep ocean and the sun beat down our backs. Strands of your hair glinted. Spun gold in nutmeg thread. With caramel sand between your toes, and stretching far behind. Our future stretched out, in front.

Tara-Jane Colligan

Forgotten Drill

If tonight I die
Please know I did try
I held out for so long
But through walls so thin
I heard the cry,
Like soft melting tin
Falling from a grey sky.

If tonight the walls bleed red
Upon the floors
Of ancient dread
Know the thoughts of terror
Were far from head
And a white feather will lie
Upon my bed.

If tonight you hear that sound
That once followed you around
You'll remember that feeling
Like sweat hitting ground.
Do know I saw your eyes fill
Like now a forgotten drill
That saw you through evil.

If tonight screams fill your mind
And the shots seem so unkind
Remember I knew you before
I saw what love was,
This came to you so pure,
I know what happened
Was not part of your chore.

If tonight guilt pulls you down
To a place where the ashes lie
And you want to drown
Rather than look fate in the eye,
Do know on that fateful night,
It was a bloody fight
And I thank you.

Mandy Ankers

Sunrise On The Bay

The sea, the sea
I love the sea
Sunlight glistens like the morning star
A gull hovers on a westward breeze,
Stars are gone now the morning's here
The hills surround the sandy bay,
Sunlight glistens and glows on the glass-like sea,
orange, pink hues with the sunrise I see
It's morning now, the night's gone away.
Salt air I breathe fresh is the air,
Sea lapping on the shore, the sun is greeting the day –
I hope I'll be blessed one day.

Susan Byers

Roses In The Snow

Fields of ice below,
That hearts have fled.
Roses in the snow,
Steady drops of red.

Blood drops from above;
An unseen blade
To forsake love,
Our vows are made.

Ravens patrol ground,
As the day closes,
Crimson all around,
Blooming red roses.

Ricky Kingshott

Dis En-Abled

Take a good look.
Yeah, that's right: it's not real
but it's a pretty good fake.
The colour almost matches the
shade of my skin.

I only ever had the one.
Yeah, I was born like this
but you don't miss what you've never had do you?
I don't really care,
just please don't stare.

Buttons are sometimes a problem
and cutting meat can be tough
but, on the whole, it's a breeze.
My wife loves the rest of me and
the kids don't notice.

It doesn't hold me back.
Yes, I can do the same things as you except
play the piano and, maybe, type.
But hey, I'm a great runner,
in fact, I'm a winner
None of us are perfect.

People struggle for lots of reasons
and there are worse things.
Lighten up! It's a sunny day, I'm warm
and the world is a wonderful place.

David Stockdale

4am

The water crashes over her, but it won't wash him away. She doesn't know why she does these things, but it's not the first time and it certainly won't be the last. Not for the man who left silently ten minutes before, not for her. She wasn't even his first tonight; as soon as she opened the door she could smell another. Cheap perfume and cheaper sex. Is this why he left for quick shags in nightclub bathrooms with young girls who are dead behind the eyes? She wasn't surprised when his name flashed up on the screen of her mobile at 4am. She'd been calling him, though that's nothing new. It's been four months now and although the warm burgundy glow of Merlot each night goes someway towards dulling the feeling, she still struggles and he knows it. He knows that if he can't face his soulless penthouse with just his own face staring back at him from mirrored surfaces and promotional posters to keep him company, he can always count on Old Jenny. Old reliable. Old faithful. Well, this geyser's about to explode. Her fists tighten as she remembers those nights sitting up waiting for him in their bed, counting down the minutes until 7am when she would rise for yet another day of scroungers and paperwork. She feels pathetic and desperate and she hates herself for it. 'I don't blame you. I do the same thing,' she'd told him, blatantly lying. There's never been anyone but him.

Alexandra Heavyside

Time

Time: constant; omnipresent, unchanging,
Never to yield or suppress; endearing,
Unconfined by limits: boundless,
It is free; unspent, continuous.
Time is ambiguous; it stands up on its hind,
Waiting for you to catch up, sit patiently behind,
The next moment, changes pace – speeds off down the street,
Where and when will you, and time again meet?
Time heals, teaches and ticks; flies, creeps and nicks,
Rolls . . . strolls . . . on by; within the blink of an eye.
A minute ticks into an hour, an hour stretched into a day,
An eternity squeezed into a second, the same it will not stay.

Long before your time did come, and long after you've passed,
Time is the one sure thing, that will forever last.

Rachel Nugent

No One Left

Fuzzy black and white specks danced in front of his vision as his eyelids struggled open. Colour seeped into his cracked vision, grey and brown walls at first, then a pool of crimson beside his head. Pushing himself off the floor he raised a hand to the throbbing pain above his ear. Muffled cracks like thunder boomed off the walls.
His eyes fell to the rifle hanging from the sling across his chest. In that same instant the earlier noises punched through the receding concussion: gunshots and screams. Suddenly John Sashmon wished he hadn't remembered where he was, or why he was there.
He staggered at the storage room's door. Before he could open the cold, metal latch Sashmon stopped himself, fear giving him pause.
Get a grip.
A comrade was in danger, and no one deserved to be left alone, not in this place. Lifting the latch Sashmon shouldered the door open, his rifle up at his shoulder as he barrelled out to the dying echo of a shot.
'Jorgen!'
He rushed out into the tunnels and soon found his comrade. As he knelt beside them he felt for a pulse. Nothing.
His fingers tightened on the rifle's grip. Sashmon clamped down on his anger, crushing it until the thought of revenge was nothing more than an ember. Getting himself killed wouldn't help anybody at this point; justice was better than revenge for the dead.
Sashmon stood, preparing to face the nightmare in the city above.

Sean Kingston

Miss Fortuna

Wimbledon strawberries and cream
A summer fortnight-long dream
That melts and trickles, like the perspiration
Pulsing beneath my shades and sunhat,
Suffocating this sevenfold speculation
Of 'It seemed so likely this time.'
On the courts, driven by vintage wine,
Saying no to the journalists' pythonesque mics,
No to their taunts that the end is in sight,
Yes to the umpire's crisp chime.
That glare in your eyes, a glimmer of frustration,
Which melts at my glance and softens to seduction,
Says – 'Come, let me induct you to my well-trodden ways
In the lusty, lustful heat of Wimbledon days.'
Miss Fortuna brings it back to deuce
And slyly bribes the enemy for truce,
Her frame flowing like water
In the measured quarter
Of the court, her eyes knives never refused.
I waited in the lobby till it ended –
Another seeded player fast upended.
She takes me in and smiles,
My arms she soon beguiles,
Her quelling lips with mine quickly befriended.
A summer fortnight's hopes speak of frustration.
Was it a nightmare or a radiant vision?
Was Miss Fortuna a mere extension of my dreams,
Which like her fade with the strawberries and the cream?

Olivia Feilden

Ode To An Angel

O Angel! Hear these tuneful Sonnets sung,
My sweet nostalgia and meditation clear,
Please excuse that thy mourning should be done,
Even into night-time, this sacred year,
Surely I was not there, but once did see
The winged spirit with glittering eyes
I floated in the forest aimlessly,
And, I saw heaven fading in disguise,
I saw her aura glow bright and wide,
In deepest space watching the glistening truth of life and tangled flowers,
where there laid,
A secret, mind inspired.
Earth rushed, like flowing waters, swirling chaos,
Clean, holy-white and growing sensation,
I lay deep-breathing in the blessed shrine,
Our soul embraced and your guidance true,
Our skin touched not, had no need to prove,
Although detached in my double vision,
You drifted through me causing our collision,
Your splendid pure-crown of mysterious state,
The winged soul, I knew,
But who was thou who shifted dreaded fate
My sadness flew O placid love and unexplained visions afar
I see paradise forming, spontaneous
Divide us quickly sacred, amber star,
Or fester, fixated with your own loss.
Higher than me, your temple mind has won,
No alter drowned with teardrops,
Nor pathway destroyed to cause malicious throne,
Amongst the twisted crops.
No mask, no flute, no bell, no increased heat
From clear ice softly melting.
No time, no moon, no oracle, we meet
You pale-faced Angel, gleaming O Goddess
Though too late for saving Earth,
Too, too late to stop hell's slumbering fire,
The devil wants to anchor holy birth,
Holy the Devil, the Angel and the shire,
I know this time you are all desire,

Your nature elegant, I truly sense,
Fluttering between my heads experience,
I cry and laugh from my own soul, inspired.
Let me be one at present, I will pass light
Upon the waxing curse, I pray, you kneel,
I preach, you sweetly sing,
You changed cosmic meaning.
Your soul, your eyes your mystery, your wings
You pale faced Angel, gleaming.
Yes, I will be your sun, your moon and reign,
In some downtrodden heaven, search your mind,
Where fire spreads, you heal my constant pain,
Fearful I am when bearing your firm pride.
Far, far around shall those bright-charged stones
Fetch the wild-dreaming snowdrops, drop by drop,
And there by heaven, lakes, and webs and clones,
The fulfilled swirling hell is forced to stop
And in the core of this shy quietness,
A pleasant description I have stressed
I have learnt lessons in a ghastly strain,
With shells and spells and traps without a name,
I see the universe vivid in my brain,
I slowly progress I'll never be the same,
And you shall be here with me for eternity,
That heavenly drought has gone,
A bright glow and a porthole into infinity,
To let my soul live on.

Gemma Hitchcock

Fog

At first there was nothing, but as she stood, vague shapes appeared around her. She turned around trying to find a definite point to fix on but the shapes came and went as a thick mist obscured them in a never-ending mystical dance. There were things that she recognised but before she could name them they were gone, lost back into the nothingness. A voice called a name. Was it calling her? Would anyone rescue her from this never-ending nightmare of confusion?

Just silence.

As she panicked, the fog grew thicker and closer. The shapes disappeared and she stumbled forward, or was it in circles? There was nothing to relate to, nothing to hold onto. She was in a blankness that stifled everything except her own ragged breathing as her brain ceased to be able to work out a way of resolving the situation. At that point her claustrophobia kicked in and she flailed her arms about in an attempt to tear through the tendrils that encircled her, pushing her down into the never-ending billowing fog.

Suddenly the fear disappeared to be replaced by a relaxing feeling of floating. Opening her eyes she saw that all the fog was below her. It was just white sheets on her bed and her pillow of fog just a pillow. A man cradled her hand. 'Welcome back, darling.'

Who was he? She tried to concentrate as the fog crept up again but it was too much effort to stay.

Sally Herbert

The Beauty In Life

Do you ever realise that life can be beautiful?
We go through life with days feeling down, stressed and tired
We don't always notice or think about the beauty in life
The good that has happened rather than the bad
The hope for the future
The haven of home
The awe of a graceful scene
The serenity and joy that comes from the right relationships
The aura of true love that becomes apparent particularly at special events
The exhausting happiness of a day out
The determination for success
The evoking of emotion from creations of the mind . . . so vast
The unbelievable glee of good news
The recognition of a talent or hard work

So many positives we could see
If we only lived more positively
A light can be found in the darkness
There is such beauty in life

Lucy Ann Smith

Fearful Is The Storm

The thunder roars with a deafening crash
The dark sky is ablaze with lightning's yellow flash
And rain in sheets comes heavily down
And the gale force wind blows all around

For now the storm has taken its menacing hold
As the temperature drops and the atmosphere feels so cold
And the trees bend and violently shake in the storm's path
As they feel the brutal force of the storm's wrath

No one can tell how long the storm will rage
Or how much destruction, devastation or damage
The storm will cause as it charges along
Fuelled by the momentum of a gale force wind

Even when the storm to a halt does grind
The gale force wind is but a breeze
What mayhem and heartbreak it leaves behind
With destruction in towns, villages and big cities too.

AV Carlin

Ashes To Ashes – An Extract

Yesterday began to converse with me, saturating my mind with strange faces. I shuddered as I attempted to expunge them from my memory but my system denied the command. My body often rejected my instructions as if it was being regulated by someone else. Sometimes it felt as if my body had been rented, I was living in borrowed space with the constant interference of a landlord. There was always something preventing me from feeling completely settled in my own body, an underlying unease rested in the subtext of everything. Even my heartbeat felt as if it was on loan, there were times when I could hear it so piercingly almost like I was outside of my own body listening in with a stethoscope.

Qurratulain Zaheer

Last

Rumblin' Bill 'n' Di-mond Jill
Have tumbled through another day
Neither too appreciative of what
Might have come their way
Alarms and emergencies were
Encountered and quelled
Amidst a bantering series
Of jokes that gelled
At last the minute hand spelled
Weary hour's end, the beast was felled.

You know if you loved me
One time; you might know what's
In my mind; it is this; that if you
Ever knew how much the
Winds of time flow; and how
Ever hard the seas storm; you will
Be mine forever when the golden
Fleece is shorne

The bus has tolled off it's passenger
With feet like lead
To wander his bleary
Way back to bed;
With shouts in the night alley
The drunken boys sing Frisco
To waken him with
Their appalling disco
Finally din dies down all round
His thoughts themselves are drowned . . .

Nicholas Aldridge

They Took Risks

'Yes,' said the Creator, 'I think I will.
Let there be light.'
And so the universe began.

'Yes,' said the old man, 'I will build that boat.
Let the rains come down, we are safe.'
And the animal kingdom was preserved.

'Yes,' said the Chaldean, 'I will relocate.
Let the journey begin.'
And a nation was born.

'Yes,' said the prince, 'I'll lead the way.
Let my people go.'
And slaves were set free.

'Yes,' said the young widow, 'I'll go with you.
Let your people be my people . . . '
And a family line continued.

'Yes,' said the shepherd boy, 'I'll get him.
Let battle commence.'
And public enemy number one was slain.

'Yes,' said the beautiful young woman, 'I'll take the risk.
Let the King show his favour upon me.'
And a holocaust was averted.

'Yes,' said the peasant girl, 'I will have your baby;
Let it be to me as you please.'
And a saviour was born.

'Yes,' said the carpenter, 'I will die.
Let me pay the price.'
And the Creator was satisfied.

Kathy Rawstron

The Sailor

Down to the beach
for a short walk
I met a stranger
and we did talk
I asked him
where he came from
He told me, 'The sea'
but there was something wrong
'How could you come
from the sea?' I said
'When man lives on land
you would be dead'
The stranger pointed
with an eerie gaze
For out to sea
and through the haze
He said he was a sailor
many years ago
But the ship he was on
had sunk deep below
Storms had been strong
his ship was sinking
All of the crew
were shouting and weeping
Sadly everyone perished
and their spirits still weep
'That's why I came to you
so we are released from the deep.'

Niall McManus

Mother's Nature

Cooling cold winter air
Frozen lakes are abound
Refreshing kiss of cold
Icicles all around

Springtime is here again
New season buds awake
The whistle song of singing birds
Together that they make

Summertime full of warmth
Is joy of nature's bloom
Essence of new coloured flowers
The earth which was their womb

Autumn leaves are changing
Yellow, red and brown
The wind moves so swiftly
To bring them down to ground

The seasons that you do enjoy
Not one but all of four
That we are ever so lucky
The changes that we saw.

Darren Bly

1975 California

Night draws curtains on the street.
November lights lamps, they glow
amber and then begin their shift.
My father and I at opposite ends
of the little room, he writes in black
fountain, curly, small letters, always
ink, always full of detail. I sit reading
'Lord Of The Rings' again and we
listen to Don and Glen as the tinkling
piano fades on 'wasted time'. Joe
slides in with his southern edge and
a foreign hotel is celebrated by two
quiet men. My dad wants to know
why they question Jesus. I am puzzled
too, it's all missionaries and Americans,
aliens to me. A tut crosses one raised
eyebrow but Dad continues to write as
the needle clicks to a finish. The glass
door creaks open and supper calls us
from the white house. Book closed,
papers folded, a son and his dad leave
the spare room. The black vinyl sits
gathering dust on sparkling grooves
and scratches regardless. The needle
sticks at the end of side two and
unbeknown to us life in California
carries on eternally.

Andrew Scotson

I Care

I feel for you in my thoughts
in my love, you who have
suffered in so many ways!
Through sickness, through sadness
it blighted all your days!

I feel for you the poor in spirit
troubled in mind depression it
stings. You will find the sweetness
of this life! May your cup be
filled may love your heart entwined!

I feel for you the homeless, in
the cold in rain trudging
endlessly many with pain, hungry
thirsty please God! Let their
light shine again! Are we!
Am I! To blame.

I feel for you in bitterness in
loneliness, comfort be by your
side, once a caring soul
with caring hand, this was never
planned.
At the end God be by your side!

June Joy

My Garden

The garden I have now is not like the one I had before,
this one is in buckets, pots, tubs and containers placed each side of my door,
But from my window I see lawns, borders and trees,
every shade of green copper and silver in-between,
against the sky ever so high stand the majestic planes,
but the most beautiful sound and sight is the bird's song and flight
they are so many I can almost touch them they are so near.
The song thrush and blackbird bring a tear, the robin and blue tit
joined by the sparrows, dunnets and little Jenny wren.
The doves and wood pigeons
even the black, black crow
all create a wonderful show,
it's as if they perform and display just for me.
This and more is what I see
even the squirrel shows no fear of me.
So although this garden is not like the one I had before
it's so beautiful and just outside my door.

M A Andrews

Who Or What?

Whose eyes are those that watch me
Yet stay out of sight
I feel them on me
Oh! – Why do they haunt at night

Why does that black shadow come
Into view when there's
Nothing here to cast a shadow
Yet it's climbing the stairs

And that creaking sound is meaningless
Cos there's no wind or draught
To make this happen
Oh! Whose voice just laughed

There's only myself in here
Yet there's the sound of
Footsteps behind me
Oh! What a night: – I'm not tough!

Ghosts, it can only be you
Why torture me so
Please stop throwing things
Won't you calm down – and please – go!

After all that I've seen
And all that I've heard
From the all-invisible
I feel I'm entitled to be scared!

Now the lights are flickering on and off
Oh! They'll plague with anything it would seem
Ah, at last morning is here and I find
It was all just a bad dream.

Snowflake

A White Night Vanished Upon Waking

Is this a story of bravery and glory, of the good health and the poorly, where good overcomes evil surely? In the night no star shined bright, no star in sight, the clouds gather up above as the cold winds bite. Now the diamond dust trickles down, like an infant's frown; then becomes a blanket as it hits the ground. Here comes the freeze, step outside you'll think, where are my knees?

High above in the thickest, thinnest trees, full of frozen leaves; that swings with the breeze, listen carefully as the branches sneeze. Look upon the frozen heavens, was midnight blue now it's grey, until night becomes day. Frost lost its bite, dark turns bright, as the smiling sun emits rays all that froze, finally finishes its melt away. So smile I say like the brightest day.

Vijay Wellington

The Message

I talked to my God last night,
When I lay alone in bed
I shared my hopes and my dreams,
Many visions, all in my head.
And I asked that in his great wisdom
He might make himself known to me,
Now this morning I surely can see him
As I gaze at the lovely country.
For the wind in its power and glory
Moves all in the sky, land and sea,
I know without my God,
This magnificence just could not be.
As the clouds move with speed and precision
The sun shows its smile, now and then,
I say thank you my Lord for this lesson,
And end with a solemn. Amen.

Penelope Turl

My Friend

Little cat – I laid you to rest in my garden by the forest.
Each month is a new beginning,

March days of wild wind will humour you to sleep.

April with her blossoms will scatter pink petals falling like rain.

May with its strong daylight will attract the butterflies like confetti and dragonflies will dance to hushed circle flight.

June you will find peace. The sun will bring you comfort – the birds will sing to their little ones – perhaps you will laugh at their innocence?

July – lazy bees will hum, spiders will spin their lace to shield you from the heat.

August – the oak tree will protect you with its strong leaves feeling cool, as ladybirds fall asleep and hedgehogs only wink.

September – has magic colours – golden leaves in the early autumn breeze will make you feel at ease – including peace.

October – little stray cat passing by her eyes looked at me as if to say, 'Can I come home with you today?'
Her purr is in tune to her dreams by my fire.

November – so dark that only nightingales sing.

December – the snow will make a shimmering light as deer shelter in the cold of the night.

January – you know I am always there where silence is the gift of death.

February – may your spirit run free like you once did – my beautiful Siamese cat,
Your velvet paws walking down the corridors of forgotten time.

Barbara Posner

The World Is Waiting

The world is waiting.
Waiting for what? Truce
For a time when there is peace.
For a world where innocent children are safe.

A world free from those who violate people's rights.
A perfect world in an unpretentious state.
But stop! And think, instead of wait
Look, see, listen, be thankful for God's free gifts we enjoy.

Seed time and harvest yield provision for our needs.
Listen to the birdsong; watch wildlife, the beauty of blooms.
It is not the world that is injudicious.
It is the insubordination of its people.

Elizabeth Moore

Snow Scene

The snow – the dramatic snow,
So transforming to all we know,
Imperfections all disappear,
Sounds fall distant to the ear.

Sometimes night frost restores the scene,
A sparkle returns once more,
In moon and starlight . . . a childhood dream,
Such a pristine vision we cannot restore.

But – as in all the things we know,
Such beauty cannot remain,
So soon all crushed and trampled below –
A brown slurry to fill each drain.

R R S Leach

War Dead

Say you won't forget us;
Now we're gone from view.
So many of us,
And so young,
But duty was to do.

Remember us in springtime;
When sunshine fills the air
And swallows grace the clear blue sky,
With ne'er a worry there.

When you picnic midst the flowers,
Remember pals with joy.
And how we splashed within the river,
As when you were a boy.

For there's nothing as strong as duty,
That brings all humans free.
Only the love of those remembered,
Within your memory.

Say you won't forget us;
We ask through tears of men.
'Tis the prayer of the fallen,
And our last wish, Amen.

Windsor Hopkins

Elgar And Malvern

A modest range of understated hills,
a British compromise of height and shape
that rises bird sharp from the Worcester plain.
An interesting skyline not too high,
accessible yet with secret ways
that suddenly surprise the visitors
with hidden beauty so they look again.
Just like his music with its sudden surge
of deep emotion underneath the calm,
in which we may see something of ourselves,
of strong convictions tempered by restraint
and with at times an enigmatic wit.
It is no wonder that he dominates
the programme of the Last Night of the Proms,
this curious mixture of sheer fun and pride
of heritage that's tinged with irony,
complexity within simplicity.
Though here the national psyche is on show,
proud flags from other countries also wave
and celebrate our shared humanity.
His music tells of Britain but much more
So at this year's Proms we welcome all,
not just with Elgar's pomp but with his soul.

Don Nixon

The Charm Of Summer

The morning dew lay so soft and new
As the day dawned with a natural calm,
And the flowers glowed with nature's hue,
Enhancing all of summer's charm.

And we strode out along the way
As the birds in the hedgerows burst into song,
And the sun shone down and warmed the day,
Whilst love really bloomed, a feeling so strong.

Yes, romance blossomed in the summer breeze,
Amidst sheer beauty and budding growth,
The swaying corn, the restless trees,
I reached out and embraced them both.

The radiance in my lovers' smile
Caused heartbeats fast, little sense of time,
Still I could tell in a short while
That I would be in life's rich prime.

For she did stir within my soul
A feeling so divine and whole,
Whence all was mine for to control,
And heaven itself shone down upon me.

Chris Norton

The Fallen

They stood knee-deep in mud and mire
Their comrades dead and dying
The fear they felt was second best
For pity in their hearts was lying

Their country was relying on them
And loved ones waited too
The battles got more fierce each day
And friends grew very few

For every hour of every day
They fought a battle through
Thousands sacrificed their lives
And heroes more than a few

So God be with each precious soul
Who stood on battle ground
In agony and torment every hour
With bodies all around

Father God this prayer I pray
That those who fight for love
Love of God, of flag, of peace
Shall dwell with you above

1914-1918
1939-1945
And all others since.

Alma Taylor

Awards And Prizes

What strangest criteria or logic was that
Were names on a list drawn out of a hat?
Presentations in secret, was that just the point,
For fear those decisions might bore, disappoint?
But best to show others inform and inspire
From achievement and effort awards may transpire.

Who wants an award of a narrow braid sash
In poor quality fabric and design a mishmash!
Much better would be a cravat or corsage
To delight and enhance a youthful visage.
Or later to buy for three pounds ninety-nine
A tie in those colours when shopping online?

On leaving school at the age of fifteen
A cookbook prize for my shot at cuisine.
Those practical prizes – and Bibles for all –
Food for body and soul, and this I recall,
Words of wisdom and truth against suffering and strife.
With a Bible and cookbook I was set up for life!

Hard work dedication there's no substitute
For success in exams there is no dispute.
With diplomas, certificates in various guises,
For attainment or progress the valued book prizes.
Then rewards at retirement that no one can knock
Fine items in glass and an elegant wall clock.

Winning in lotteries, draws and in competitions
With ability, skills or plain intuitions.
From failures the confidence may take quite a knock,
But determined effort more doors will unlock.
So of life must this be well understood
To take the bad as well as the good.

Christine Ann Moore

Family Memories

Old age steal not that which is mine,
Treasured memories of love divine,
My childhood family, affectionate, kind,
Mum, Dad, sister and brothers
Oh how I wish they were still here.
I recall steps taken to teach right from wrong,
Their love expressed on the melody of a song.
Never a curse nor swear word did they on us spit,
Nor as punchbags were we constantly hit.
If there is life to be gained on high
I pray they have a cosy nest in the sky.

Audrey Luckhurst

Tears

Moments from thunder, the sky is grey,
Wanting of a better day,
Umbrella skies to soak the pain,
The thunder roars blessed with rain.

From inside my window I watch the storm,
Dry and snug, sat in the warm.
A flash of white, the atmosphere sets,
Contemplating choices, not want to regret.

My tears are falling with the rain
As it rolls down the windowpane,
A clap of noise coincides with my pain,
Lightning follows as it continues to rain.

I shut out the night and close my eyes,
The sun welcomes me as I rise.

Mark Gittings

The Ancient Academic

The ancient academic
In her blue and white print frock
With her
White hair all escaping round her head –
Every day she rides her bicycle
Through the hallowed streets of Cambridge
And thinks about her
Fellow students
Some still living
Most long dead.

Upon Midsummer Common
On a blanket on the ground, she sits
To eat her sandwiches
And to drink a flask of tea.
She recalls her time at Girton
Where she studied maths
And English literature
And played croquet on Sundays
And learned to drive a car.

She trundles through the hippy stalls
Of Strawberry Fair
In June
She listens to the music
And tries food from many lands
She wears an old straw hat
To keep the sunshine from her eyes
And buys
Silver rings and bracelets
To decorate
Her wrinkled hands.

She takes herself to Parkside
Where the policemen drink their tea
And where the fire brigade next door await the bell
She crosses through the rushing traffic
And she heads towards the pool
So she can get her twenty lengths in
Front and back
And side as well.

She wanders round the 'Grafton'
Through its modern shops and precincts
And thinks back to 'The Kite'
It used to be
And later on at Drummer Street
She boards the bus for Histon
There to
Meet a friend of long acquaintance
Go to church, and stop for tea.

Through Lion Yard to the market
With its stalls and coloured awnings
Where the happy costa mongers
Sell their wares
To a book fair in the Guild Hall
On the upper floor she wanders
Pausing to catch her breath
As she slowly climbs the stairs.

She celebrates her birthday
With a party in 'The Orchard'
Just a few old pals at Grantchester
Now that she is 85
She travels there by 'Panther'
(A taxi is a treat for her)
And sits upon a deckchair
And eats
Chocolate cake in the sun.

She cycles to the station
And she gets a train to Ely
And then to the great cathedral
Makes her way.
The hushed and echoed voices
Fill the air with quiet simplicity
And she sits in the refectory
And she eats cheese scones
And prays.

She knows the many seats of learning
All the colleges of the city
She knows them well
And loves them all the same
She knows each faculty
Each department
They are her family
And her life
She was only ever to be a student
And sadly
Never to be a wife.

The ancient academic
In her blue and white print frock
With her white hair all escaping round her face
Rides her bicycle
Down Victoria Road
And makes her way to Girton
To the little house
Which she has made her place.

Her sisters all got married
And raised families of their own
But not she
For she wanted more from life
But for a higher education
She had to make a sacrifice
And governed by society
Had to choose to be a student – or a wife.

Not *both* for her
Unlike today
She had to make a choice
Was forced to separate two loves she had.
One for the dashing soldier boy
One for the need to learn
And each one
Burnt a hole within her heart.

And so
She bid farewell to Tom
One cold day long ago
And took the train to Cambridge
Far away
Her bright new home in Girton
Took her far amongst the stars
And it is there that she
Still resides today.

Kathryn Critchley-Fowler

Nature

It is the demonstration of grace
within the conceptual framework of science
and nature as we understand it.
Self realisation is born and matures
in the highest subjective essence of life.
We are guided by our mental powers,
as we endeavour to remain faithful and loyal.
Being rooted in a distinctive awareness
that is our purpose to love,
pursuing a course that is not burdensome
but trustworthy.

Kizzy Hawker

The Blackbird

As I strolled out one morning,
With nature to commune,
I heard a blackbird singing,
How lovely was his tune.
And in that summer morning,
The dew still on the ground,
I listened to the blackbird,
And marvelled at the sound.
How prodigal I thought him,
With his melody,
For not once he sang it,
But on repeatedly.
Soon others joined his singing,
It seemed from everywhere,
But of all the birds that,
Sang with him,
His was the sweetest air.
Through fanciful the notion,
The thought occurred to me,
That it was for me alone,
He sang his melody.
But it was just for himself,
He with rapture sang his song,
It was his way of welcoming,
The coming of the dawn.

Edward McCartney

Off-Key

Between Facebook, Twitter and the email
we hadn't really spoken for a while,
but after downing shots we ended up together
in good old-fashioned office party style.

The artificial Xmas tree stood mocking
when I dislodged your artificial hair;
a fake fingernail was severed in a zipper,
a smart phone dunked in vodka for a dare.

I can't remember too much now I'm sober,
but your spray tan left a stain that won't come out;
two false eyelashes are lurking in my duvet,
it was only lipstick formed your lips into that pout.

I led you to believe that I was wealthy
and in my thirties, but I'm forty and the joke
is that the car outside is now owned by my ex-wife,
the flat's on loan, the watch a fake and I am broke.

You looked disgusted by my overhanging belly –
I used to be a well toned virile guy;
between the bald patch and my bad back life seems harder,
I seldom see my son and sometimes cry.

If I pass you on the street one rush hour morning
or you fail to recognise me on the train,
I could email an apology by lunchtime,
you could text me within minutes to explain.

If we were standing here together right this second,
I doubt we'd spare each other the time of day,
but check our schedules for a window and smile briefly,
take a rain check and then quickly walk away.

Jill Parker

The Creator

I wait and watch from the shadows
I whisper your name through the wind in the trees
I am the sunlight that warms your face
The moon that watches you sleep
The stars that light your way
The birds that sing you awake
The perfume that evokes your nostrils as you breathe
in the scent of a flower
I am the butterfly that fluttered close
as you prayed
I am in everything that you see
I am your creator
I love you.

Diane Mills

A Post-Mod Rake's Progress

Garish lipstick, glaring eyes, customised cars
extravagantly-coloured 'small differences of taste'.
Grayson parodies Hogarth's 'hero' as ingenu geek –
smart phones clamour, decors shout 'admire!'
Grandparents downsized to kind-faced observers
of their offsprings' self-caricatures:

Geek Tim's software earns wealth, blonde-girl and ancient
mansion where a monster-stag declares the decay
of 'class': 'Rich is Bad' 'Tim pay your Tax'.
Hubris comes with the crash of his scarlet Ferrari:
her Gucci bag's rubbished, she's bereft; his end is bloody,
dark reds, harsh pinks, cops; the humiliating undress
of death, in a black stranger's arms, echoing Christ.

Olga Aryamati

Nothing To Pay

I think I'm very lucky
As I never pay for food
I couldn't afford the prices
They would charge to feed my brood. (8 of us!)
No one is allowed to be fussy
We will eat anything going
I'm hanging round the garden now
As the man next door is mowing. (Thinks worms!)

Got a beak full of worms for dinner
Would be nice to find some bread
Then we could have a sandwich
Before we think about bed.

In return for our meals
We will keep your garden neat
It's time to make my exit now
Here comes the patter of feet (I mean paws!)

Grateful Sammy sparrow.

Brenda Bartlett

Racing To Summer

It is a conjuration as much as anything.
An awakening of steam commands
each fire born part of this beast
to flex and heave together,
biting hard rails as it lurches
towards us from the dank past.

Our lazy Sundays are a doddle for this giant.
Built for the long haul,
these jaunts to Hemingfield are small beer.
Stationed between punters, it dreams of the main line.

The full throttle adventure of spring fields racing to summer.

Tony Noon

Now And Then

Stones,
Flung in the sun at tinting leaves, with
Conkers drop,
Sheaves shining harvest done;

In shade,
Sticks made to thrash boughs in glee's delight,
Swinging and rocking, summer turning,
Autumn come.

New boys
Branches shake and swinging branches break; with
Squeal or fight taking a licking for
Tradition's sake.

Bullies sport
Never to repeat or cry, retreat, retort, with
Fists illogic drumming
Teach; and

Conkers take a whacking:
'One-er' 'Two-er' 'Three-er' 'Strings'
In the yard rings, ties
Never severed.

Bronze memories cradled in the palm,
Talismen,
Prickly pods winking, luscious as
Girls' eyes.

Alas, 'Agonner',
All 'Agonner'.

Now,
Burnt-out candles cling,
Still, to swinging branches,
Develop pods.

And boys,
Exams done, muscle-up to stand alone, term come,
In good hands horse chestnuts
Conquer.

Pods winking
Wait.

Oliver Cox

The Money Tree Policy

'Oh no
my bank's gone bust.
What about my hundred quid?'
'Oh no
my bank's gone bust.
What about my million quid?'
'It's okay,' says the government of, for and by the people.
'That's what we're here for.'
'Thank God,' says the man with a hundred quid.
'Thank God indeed,' says the man with the million quid.
'Trouble is,' says the man from the treasury.
'It's going to cost each and every one of us ten thousand quid
over the next five years.'
'That sounds like a lot,'
Says the man who stood to lose a hundred quid.
'Oh well, I suppose I'll live,'
Says the man with nine hundred and ninety-nine thousand quid
pro
quo
In the bank.

Alan Harman

The Circus

Today I went to the circus
I'd never seen one before
I slowly approached the enormous tent
And then I heard the lions roar.

Joining the queue, I went inside
Amazed at what I could see
The ringmaster stood in his shiny red coat
He seemed to be looking straight at me.

In came the jugglers, one by one
Throwing balls in the air, higher and higher
They finished their act in spectacular style
Catching sticks that were all afire.

The horses next with pretty red plumes
Came trotting by in a graceful way
The foal kept getting left behind
I think he really wanted to play.

Now it was time for the elephants
Each one holding the other one's tail
And right at the end was the baby
Compared to the others, he looked very frail.

Suddenly a cage appeared
And out came all the big cats
The trainer came and cracked his whip
Slowly the lions and tigers all sat.

Onto the stool, then down again
Through the hoops, the crowd wanted more
But every time the whip was cracked
They always responded with a roar.

A roll of drums and a gasp was heard
And a light appeared in the sky
At the top of the tent they'd hung a wire
All at once my mouth was dry.

With a pole in his hand he started across
I couldn't watch, I closed my eyes
I opened them up, he was almost there
Then, 'He's there, he's there,' I heard the cries.

They all appeared at the end of the show
Jugglers and clowns together
The animals paraded around and around
The ringmaster looked at the end of his tether.

I said goodbye to the circus today
They'll be back next year to see us
I will remember all of my life
The day that I went to the circus.

Barry Winters

Just For A Time

If I could once again hold you, just for a time
I would let you know how I long for you to be mine.
If I could once again speak to you, just for a time
I could make you understand how deeply I loved you.

Though now you are gone and I am left to reflect on what once was.
I yearn to be near you, even just for a time
So you could see,
that you belong with me.

Though time has run too short,
Forever from now, I'll wonder what could have been,
If only my love for you, you could have seen,

Were it not just for a second, just for a moment,
Just for a time.

Lewis Cavanagh

Boris The Toothless Beaver

There once lived a beaver called Boris, who was born without any teeth,
He sucked on the leaves and the bark of the trees, he then hid in his dam underneath

Poor Boris was very unhappy, he longed to chew wood like the others,
To gnaw down big trees, with the greatest of ease, just like his sisters and brothers

His family all knew that he struggled, so Dad called a meeting one day,
He gathered the creatures together, and this is what he had to say

'Our Boris is so sad and lonely, he feels like he's always left out,
He can't eat his food good and proper, of that there can be not one doubt'

So the colony all clubbed together, with the ducks, the voles and the otters,
And bought poor young Boris, the shiniest pair of ***enormous*** false beaver choppers!

The family and friends got together, as the gift had arrived for young Boris,
All beautifully wrapped by his sister, (with help from her duck friend called Doris)

Dad, he then shouted out, 'Boris! I've got something here, just for you!'
'OK Dad, I'm coming,' cried Boris, 'just give me a minute or two'

Boris then wandered out slowly and said, 'Why is everyone here?'
His dad said, 'We thought you'd like these mate, so now you can eat with no fear'

All the family and creatures cheered loudly, as Boris then popped in his choppers,
'Thank you so much,' he said, overjoyed. 'I can now give our Brian back his loppers'

Boris is now so, so happy, he gnaws down the trees with such pride,
He met a young beaver called Betty, who soon would become his new bride.

Claire Bowl

Special Moments

Feeling your touch on my neck I feel at ease.
Can I feel your lips kissing my neck, feel your coldness against my body.
Laying there my love for you is strong, afraid to move, want to saviour your touch.
Your hands brush through my hair, twirling and caressing with care.
Lips brush against my cheeks, feel your body against my back.
Your touch so cold, though that I know.
Scared to turn around, want to hold onto this special moment.
Always loved you from your head to your toes.
Caving in I turn around, though you're not there
You passed away a while back, still I'm sad.
I sometimes feel you in the room with me, yet I cannot see you.
Special moments like that, I hold dear to my heart.
Always in my dreams, cuddling at the seams.
Wishing you were here with me, I don't know what to say.
You blew me away, I think and love you every day.
Never forgotten, always with me, guiding and protecting me.
Will never love again as you were my first my last.
My partner, my wife, my best friend.
I love you my dear till the very end.

Grant McLauchlan

Hello

The birds are singing false springs new dawn
Each good morning answers with more
good morning song,
their world exists among the chimney stacks
all give warning to next-door's tabby cat
slowly my room fills with azure blue
the musky scent reminds me that
I really should call you,
Still memories of days forlorn
Becalmed by mankind's need to adorn.

Jorj

Secrets Of Inner Peace

Learning the art of forgiveness
Is a part of the secrets of inner peace
If you can learn to forgive
Then you can begin to love again
If you understand the wrong
That has been afflicted against you
Then you can begin to trust again
So the secrets of inner peace
Is to walk hand in hand
With your virtues
Tolerance, patience, hope
Faith and others
Use them if you have to
Let them be your guide to inner peace
If you are feeling down
Let faith get you through the day
Peace of body, mind and soul
Is a wonderful feeling in itself
So reach out to your virtues
Understand how they work
Draw every ounce of strength
That you can
And make it worth while for you.

Carolie Cole Pemberton

December Oak, Church Common, Wenhaston Suffolk

Your leaves are brown
Just a few lingering touches of yellow-green
But mostly brown and many still attached
Though there is a deep carpet
Of leaves, acorn and empty acorn cups
Spread around you.
Again it is a glorious day
Blue skies and sunshine
Accompanied by a stiff, keen breeze.
As I stand beneath you
Your dry leaves scrunch and crackle
As I scuffle my feet in delight,
Overhead your thinner branches
Stir in the chilly wind,
Remaining leaves rustling and sighing
Whispering and shushing
Reminding me of the to and froing of the tide.
And so the rhythm of the year ebbs and flows
Summer, autumn, winter
With the promise of spring to come
As certain as your certainty
As certain as your Creator.

Anne Munday

Mandy

As Martin drove, many people pointed at him looking puzzled, amused or even disgusted.
He was in Mandy, his transporter, that had a striking vintage, psychedelic look.
Mandy had been modernised however and was capable of automated self drive.
Virtually everyone considered driving as a pointless and time wasting activity.
Instead people slept, played games, read or even had sex whilst self drive transporters took them effortlessly to their destinations and then manoeuvred into tight parking spaces.
As driving was Martin's hobby and passion though, he always chose to do it for himself.

Before self drivers there had once been so many deaths on the roads through over crowding, accidents and incidents of road rage that installing a system to calm drivers had been made a legal requirement.
Mood calmers gradually faded from use once automated drivers had become the norm and had eliminated accidents.

Martin though of course had never lost his love of Mandy's mood altering system.
He especially liked tricking it into thinking he really did have constant road rage because then soothing music would start playing and calming colours would light up her interior.
As he had been able to programme the calmer, he had chosen flower power music and muted colours in psychedelic patterns similar to those painted on Mandy's exterior!
It had taken Martin a while to realise what others had long believed, he should have been a child of the 1960s not of the 2060s.

Pam Higgins

The Confessions Of A Desperate Housewife

Words breathe on your oyster cheeks
with the weight of cold granite,
making cracks on velvet skin, where ripples once flowed.
You smash a metal spoon against the chipped China
of the bowl you brought, because the origami boats that grazed the crests of turquoise porcelain
reminded you of Poseidon, who was quicksilver. Now they drowned, in your half-eaten,
milk-sodden Weetabix. And just like that you said, 'Everything is ruined.'
Impure eyes, marked with red railway tracks, half-covered behind jaded hands
showed tossing and turning in hot crumpled bed sheets
torn from their corners and collecting in the middle,
so you're jolted awake because your supple arms
were scratched by barbed mattress lines.
The glorified stone, poised on a callused finger, made you cringe.
You watch me laugh, a red party balloon popped by the head of a pin
falsetto echo across whitewashed walls, settles
in the folds of your stiff suit, the one I got for you.
I can point out the fuchsia coloured lipstick stains,
that linger on your skin, long after you crept on marbled floors,
towards that holy tap, to scrub off the impurities of last nights,
'Business calls, dear!'
Meanwhile, I am left in the kitchen, scrubbing away a mess of my own,
last night's dinner, the smell of home-cooked lasagne,
stained the otherwise pristine worktop,
an ugly blood-orange blob, seeping in-between brush-stroke cracks.

Holly Lamb

Gypsy Girl

It is the night of all nights, a celebration thrives
There be music playing and fire ablaze
A night to remember for all of our lives
As the cold season changes to more hazy days.

The stars shining bright in the dark evening sky
Our people are singing high spirits they feel
Bonfire is burning and catching the eye
As we gather to give thanks for a bountiful meal.

We bask in the glory of love from our kin
As chant follows chant we remember our past
Sacred lessons, magics locked deep within
Hoping that time doesn't fly by too fast.

Swirling and smiling I dance to the tune
The violin coaxing my dark feral soul
I whisper my blessing and thanks to the moon
As deep in the music I become whole.

But all too soon the fire becomes ember
As people begin to leave this place
This is a night I will always remember
I sit by the fire a smile on my face.

One more glance at the embers, I make my way
Back to my wagon of scarlet red
Weary from dancing my body to lay
On the welcoming comfort of my bed.

But down in the shadows of the old willow tree
Deep in the darkness I see something move
A voice on the breeze is calling to me
It resonates softly my heart it does soothe.

'Come to me now, come to me here . . .
My gypsy girl dancer, my beautiful muse.
Come to me now . . . you have nothing to fear
I wish for your company, you've nothing to lose.'

His voice is like velvet, so temptingly so
Is this but a dream, will I wake up soon?
My feet silent footsteps as forward I go
To the stranger that waits for me under the moon.

A dream such as this one cannot ignore
I take his hand as he stands by the tree
'Oh my wild flower, oh how I adore
That's right petit cheri, now come to me.'

Standing beside him he breathes in my presence
Then lovingly touches my dark raven hair
My body it yields with sweet evanescence
With sweet honey smile he lays my soul bare.

'A pledge we shall make, in blood lies the key . . .
Give me your hand and be still your heart
Promise me wild fire, your love give to me
Knowest this now we shall never part.'

My body it weakens I fall to my knees
His shadow embraces like a soft gentle kiss
The flame of my life snuffed out in the breeze
Tumble down slowly in kaleidoscope bliss.

To rise once again, new born in his arms
I look into the soul of my new found love
This gypsy girl dances with newly born charms
As the raven devours the innocent dove.

Dee C Glenn

Untitled

When one day the hordes came by,
To look upon the world and sigh,
They found it wanting by and by.

And when they tried to make it right,
They stood their ground and they did fight,
For what they saw to be in sight.

Never did their heads begin,
To see that they'd made it thin,
Only causing such a din.

The chaos it came and took them all,
Enveloped them within its shawl,
the plans they'd made did only fall.

For they looked hard again,
These sad hordes of men,
At what there was to be seen then.

Beneath all the heaps of mess,
And pocketfuls of deep distress,
They found that they were blessed.

And as the hordes ebbed away,
Going from the light of day,
They had, but one solitary word to say . . .

Sara Moss

Into The Dark

As darkness falls, I appear to be in a faraway land,
where demons capture and take hold of my hand.
They call, they hunt, drain emotion from their prey,
taking the innocent ones from a golden day.

The darkened shadows scatter across a moonlit sky,
the screams I call 'Don't let me die.'
'Why are you taking me? What do you want?'
'We're the demons of the night, we pray and we hunt.'

Their teeth are almost dazzling as they capture my soul,
using my emotions and taking control.
Draining me of my energy I want to get out,
they've emptied my body, I can't even shout.

Stealing the powers that belong within me,
these demons are draining all that I used to be.
I lay there scared in the still of the night,
as the evil demons shriek in delight.

Their fearsome howls echo through the black of the night,
I feel helpless and alone, fading from sight.
The wind in the distance whispers all over the trees,
darkened shadows crawl across stormy seas.

Away into the land of the dead and unknown,
where sun, stars and life have never shone.
As I open my eyes I fall into lonely silent cries,
I wipe the teardrops from my unbelieving eyes.

As the memory of the night returns to my head,
I realise I've spent the night with the living dead.

Gail Stewart

The King And His Merry Band

On top of his castle the king stood one day
Surveying his glorious land
Such a fine summer's morn, it was, on that day
The castle stood gleaming and grand.

All the king's court to the village went they
To witness a fair maiden wed
Merrily and sprightly the band led the way
To enliven the village ahead.

The courtiers all followed the music parade
But dillied and dallied behind
The sound of the band then started to fade
They went down a dark path unsigned!

The band up ahead continued to play
The forest was dark'ning around
Their companions were wand'ring miles the wrong way
They knew not and made merry sound.

On the low road they ambled and danced
Banging and singing and fluting
When the outlaws, like lightning, sudd'nly pranced
Stabbing and hitting and shooting!

They were cut down and felled till the road ran red
There was slicing and blasting and stealing
With evil all done, the outlaws were fed,
They ran through the forest, trees concealing.

And now with the outlaws away with their fill
The music was stopped with great silence
The whole band laid dead, their bodies all still
Robbed of all life with such violence.

But never again, thought the Lord up on high
Will the valleys and courts of his land
Be so full and happy and echo and cry
With the sweet joyous sound of his band.

'Those wretched fiends yonder will suffer my wrath,
For slaughtering all of my band!
Come here my captain and put down your broth
Take all your men to the wood-land.'

Hundreds and hundreds of men he did send
Into the valleys with sword
To scour and hunt and fiercely up-end
The forests and towns for that horde.

So quiet and sad were the villages then
The soldiers and horses wept too
For the beauteous sound of the dead music men
Was instead just a cow and its moo.

The outlaws were found and were soon in the gaol
The instruments came next on horse
The band then were laid to rest without fail
And all wanted justice of course.

'Learn now to play as a band you outlaws!
For years will you toil without break
Practise and play all the day without pause
Till as fine a band as the dead one you make!'

Many years passed and a sweet sound they made
Standing in court, what a band!
Oh what great music they lovingly played
They cried at the pain done the land.

They wept at the joy they gave to the folk
Who were crying and smiling all around
They smiled at their smiles and were under no yoke
The new merry band loved their sound.

Then swift as a falcon the guardsman did fly
Shackling them all to their flutes
'What is your game, O King?' they did cry
They were bound from their lutes to their boots.

'Off with your ears!' the king he decreed
And with hot knives the soldiers stood primed
'Blind us instead, good king' they did plead,
'For our glorious sound is for all us enshrined.'

'Now will you learn what evil you did
Forever you'll play music sweet
Nought will you hear, till by death you're all rid
And my merry band you'll ne'er unseat.'

J.W. Brigden

The Poppy

In Flander's Fields the poppy grew
Future significance nobody knew
Remembrance, colour, vibrant red
For those soldiers, fallen, dead

Wars they fought, we'll never forget
But battles, conflicts, not over yet
So for the fallen in a foreign land
A poppy whose colour is like sand

Worn for Remembrance, worn with pride
A poppy of red, by its side
Worn with love, wet with tears
On the wars rage, just different years

The poppies colour does not detract
Thoughts of the fallen, that's a fact
In Afghan fields, the poppy grows
Future significance nobody knows.

Amanda Crowden

The Landscape

As the seasons change new life grows on the trees
A slight summer breeze rustles the leaves
Looking around at the wondrous landscape
My heart fills up with new desires and taste

I turn back towards the city
See all the lights shining with clarity
A small smile spreads across my face
When I think about what the world offers to the human race.

Kiran Batool Khan

Glad To Be A Dalek

I'm not your average Dalek, you know the sort I mean,
All bent on domination; giving vent to all that spleen.
I like to think I'm different from other Dalek crew,
Who keep emotions hidden while exterminating you.
I don't agree with killing, with plans to subjugate.
The universe is lovely and I find it hard to hate.
In fact, I've got my own plan; I'm working from within!
I'm teaching other Daleks how to knit and sew and spin.
I run a secret workshop, where Daleks can relax
And find their inner Dalek; get the monkey off their backs.
We try to be creative; to make things, not destroy.
I run a Dalek choir learning Ludwig's 'Ode To Joy'.
So if you see a Dalek in home-knit wool poncho,
Don't run off in a panic, come across and say 'Hello!'

Jonathan Humble

Night-Time Prowler

Quiet night, everyone asleep
Through the door padded feet creep
A sniff here and there, to no avail
So up in the air goes his furry tail
He sees that there's nobody at home
So starts to ascend the staircase, all alone
Going from this bedroom then to that
Must get it right mustn't make a flap
Ah yes, this seems to be the one – just let's see
And squeezes through the doorway, so silently
Then jumps up on the bed and curls into a ball
And hopes like everyone else (who is sleeping), not to be disturbed at all.

Barbara Coward

Queen Of The Underdog

(For DNA)

I could spend a lifetime with you
Without the lust and social buggery
That comes with every deshabille sunrise
Soft crystalline nerves
Soaked in worthless desire
Upon the wayfarer's return
Avenged my queen with that first sip of freedom
A single hair from the underdog's back
Gone all the romance of gentry I say
Hail shoe shiners garnished in greed
No pity beyond your temptation
As unchained are your chiefs of relief
Oh mother of reason between endless wars
In faith stands an amnesty to the world you were born
Burst is the bubble to a silence last drop
Falling into a glass where the ripples all stop.

Deadboy

Why Worry

At times we all have problems and we don't know where to turn
perhaps it's then we feel alone and for some help we yearn
Instead of losing sleep at night when problems multiply
There's someone who is always there on whom we can rely.

We can share our thoughts with God and ask his help in a prayer
as we put our trust in him he saves us from despair.
So many times we worry when there's nothing to be feared
Then later on we realise those problems disappeared.

Sylvia Quayle

Fires And Flames

It's always fire that gets the blame
Never the ones who ignite the flames
Like the government funded initiatives; igniting flames of hatred
But instead of being banned; it's spread, accepted and even celebrated

The wolves at the top selecting our fittest to fight
In wars they didn't start, where they risk losing their lives.
Cult leaders spewing poison-laced sermons to their congregations
Creating kids with fire up their arses, picket signs in their hands and being forced to sing anti gay songs

When the truth of the gospel is: God is love.
We've got to stop spreading fires ignited from them up above.
Cos it's corruption you see, they ignite the fires then stand back and watch
As we become their infected, blistered, flaming, chargrilled flock

Branded like cattle, by the markings of their vicious scolds
And before we realise it, we've got smoke choking our sold-out souls
And it's always the fire that gets the blame
Never the ones who ignite the flames

So next time you feel your soul is on fire
Let it be from a burning passion inside ya.
Burn bold and bright and let the furnace roar
And like iron, create something, solid, strong and pure
And remember if following the orders of another
You ensure that the fires they ignite sit well within ya

Don't allow yourself to become another dangerous arsonist
By spreading hate fuelled fires ignited by the 'elitists'
Cos to the elitists as they are often called
You're just a pawn in their game of lies, fires and wars

And it's always the fire that gets the blame
Never the ones who ignite the flames
So be true to yourself and the fires within you
Because those are the fires you are born to attend to.

Ms Anamoli Meraki

Bully

That boy you called 'Gay boy Gay!'
In the school lunch hall today
Well done. You helped him decide
He went home. Committed suicide

That girl you screamed 'Slag' to
Was it something you had to do
She won't go out. She's a virgin
And now she's started drinking gin

That boy you said was a waste of space
After school he goes home double pace
Gets ready. Goes to work till late tonight
So that his family can eat right

That girl you pushed to the ground
Hit the floor, but didn't make a sound
Did you expect her to blow a fuse
She goes home to her father's abuse

The old man selling flags in the park
You make fun of his facial scars
He's a better man than you'll ever be
He got them fighting for his country

Today you decide to make fun of me
I think it's time for you to see
I'm sat in class, I can't stop crying
Because my mum is at home dying

The one thing you really need to see
Is that you're not big, clever or funny
What made you this way? C'mon tell me
There's nothing good about being a bully.

Andrew East

PTSD And Me

My mind is fit to burst
With all that cannot be reversed
I no longer have any thirst
For a life that appears cursed

I did not have a choice
I could not find my voice
Hence succumb to the lure of death
Inhale no more painful breath

The mind's capacity to cope
Does not have endless scope
To survive reigns supreme
But happiness it cannot redeem

A state where living is a chore
The pain, it will pour
Through my body like rain
Until control is ascertained

Control in the form of severance
From sense and intelligence
Internal instinct holds the power
My sense of self it will devour

My only hope is to claw it black
Launch an attack
That reclaims my life
Shows them who holds the knife

The knife that can end it all
Instead I crawl
Do whatever it takes
Raise the stakes

Do not relinquish control
Reassemble my broken soul
That is my only hope
Without it, down I slope.

Murron McRae

A Song Of My Beloved

I am yours, my beloved,
And you are mine, my darling.

My love grows like a vine,
Stronger, all the day to you.
The flowers have blossomed,
The fruits, they have grown. Sun shone
And the rain, it has drenched.

Intertwined, yes, we are.
Only our roots are different.
Our being interlocked.
None can distinguish, you, me,
Beautiful oneness. Us.

Some seasons have crushed us,
But, dear, these have brought fine wine.
Sweet, intoxicating,
Full-bodied, choice wine of love,
My sweetheart, partner, friend.

I am yours, my beloved,
And you are mine, my darling.

A mighty stag, you are.
Beautiful, majestic, strong,
Masculine and handsome.
Sure-footed, steady, solid:
You lead me on in grace

I, your beautiful doe,
Your graceful deer, follow you.
Staying close to your path
I will follow where you go,
My lovely, my dearest.

We climb the mountain tops
Breathing in fresh air all round,
Admiring every view.
Each valley faced together
My stag protecting me.

I am yours, my beloved,
And you are mine, my darling.

May I be your heart's seal,
May my heart be on your sleeve.
For love is as strong as death.
Many waters cannot quench,
The floods do not drown love.

Love demands our gifts,
It is worth more than all wealth.
To you I give my all,
To you I give my dear love.
Set me as your heart's seal.

I am jealous for you.
My desire is you alone,
My beloved, my husband.
Drape your banner over me,
May it be one of love.

I am yours, my beloved,
And you are mine, my darling.

Penelope Page

Tunnel Vision

Midnight on the nocturnal thoroughfare,
I saw all the painted faces there
Lost! Behind digital instruments they hide,
Behind exclusive LCD monitors
They were blind.
Among 100 mutual friends they forgot
The smooth touch of the sensitive
Membrane holding this show together and apart.
With muffled hearts they recorded
Dumb expression and fed greedy palms
By misguised fantasies published in papers
Never printed and half read.
They become half human, half short-wave receiver,
Unquestioning believers of yesterday's virtual trend.
Like canned worms they twist and bend,
Evading the natural code which deserves
Such subterranean splendour. Half-hearts linger
In static gloom and peel from each other
As stung lovers on a night otherwise
Crystal and fair.

Orlando Piper

The Village War Memorial

When my pals enlisted so did I
Marching away with heads held high
Full of patriotic pride
I remember how my mother cried

Into the trenches, those muddy hells
Bombarded by bullets and mortar shells.
John, Willie and Tom all died
While Charlie and Joe and I survived
Until the next morning it came to pass
We awoke to the stench of the chlorine gas
That yellow, sulphurous, poisonous fog
Creeping over the muddy bog
That filled the eyes and mouths and lungs
Of Charlie and Joe who both succumbed
While I, half blind with tears and pain
Stumbled across no man's plain
Holding up my rifle high
I shouted curses to the sky
Then broke into a frenzied run
Straight into the sights of the sniper's gun.

Falling flat upon my face
In that God forsaken foreign place
My very last thought before I died
I remembered how my mother had cried.

Maureen Reynolds

The Looking Glass

It shows you what you really are
It shows your face near and far
It's a glass,
A sheen,
Of non-emotion
Its stare a sweep of pure devotion
To you?

It says it's for the good of you
It says it shows you to you
Like two new people every day
The mirror shows us the way

Gods can't hide it,
Neither can we,
We are all in the mirror,
We are all what we see

Beauty is in the eyes of the beholder
But beauty here will burn and smoulder,
It shapes us,
It forms us,
The devil's tool is what I speak
A vanity mirror for the weak.

George Smith

River Lark Banks In Spring

To smell the dampness, and admire
the fronds of weeping willows –
that is a sight to heave a sash
window up, with springtime panache,
for clear skies, or greying cloud-billows.

This is a splendid morning for
steering little canoes along
the Lark, from here to Barton Mills.
Though it won't offer many spills
to boaters, unless their wobble's wrong!

Dragon and damsel flies cavort
among reeds in a Monet-esque
landscape; where rowboats may be moored,
and picnic victuals hauled off board –
These scenes render Suffolk picturesque.

Gillian Fisher

Cold

I am the softest of the soft,
The whitest of the white,
Silent as the night,
I go where the wind doth blow,
Silently I come and silently I go,
I am the snow.

Tony Ellis

Dream In Colour

If a picture speaks a thousand words
How many does a dream?
If your heart speaks but goes unheard
How long before it screams?

And it screams . . . 'Listen to me'
Let go of your fears so that you can be free
Project your ideas of colourful imagery
Wipe away tears so you'll see with clarity

And those tears can separate light like a prism
Like birthing idealistic thoughts into realism
Realise your potential through wisdom
You're an individual don't worry about plagiarism

Or plagiarising
Just close your eyes and
Fall into a deep sleep

Comprising of colours
Arising from your mind's eye

Blue, sapphire the sky is your limit
Navy is truth, blue is youth, dream in it

Add red to your choice
Your inner voice says, 'Do it'
Pumping, pounding, put your heart into it
Power, passion, let your fire fuel it

Fuel your dreams and follow your dreams
Add some white, followed by cream
Envision a future of unity and peace
One where herbs cured every disease
And rich companies stopped being thieves
And stopped trying to ban natural remedies
Please!

My dreams need a bit of black
Authority
Need discipline to stay on track
Priority
Rebuke those who hold me back
Minority
Those who think alike, I attract
The majority

Did you know that your daughter's shall prophesy?
Your young men shall see visions and philosophy
Old men dream dreams, pineal eye
What are you capable of, if you tried?

I don't know if it's orange
But I hope our future's bright
View it through a kaleidoscope
And watch the colours unite

Don't view your life as film noir
Instead see it as a rainbow of colour
Don't see the world in shades of grey
Instead dream it better every day.

RochelleLoRo

All Change

So much the same
and yet so much that is not.
From just married flat with its traffic noise,
to cupboard space for countless toys,
to country quiet for old age – joys.

The home base evolves to fit
the circumstances

The first to know,
to relish children's voices –
cottage nestling amid those peaceful lanes.
Offers pushchair walks, toddler games.
It's miles way from work place aims.

Time flies and the tension builds
as school approaches.

Now it's living
just a gull's cry from the sea.
Sand and play, swimming with the tides,
watching as the toy boat glides.
Those special treat donkey rides.

The same-but-different people
using the home space.

A girl, a boy
relishing life differently.
We share this house with ghosts of its odd past,
plus sounds of top ten's furious blast
– friends filling the rooms thick and fast.

Dreams and ambitions and hopes
swirl through the ether.

Coming and going
the world beckons them.
Fresh take on village life in this new base:
shops, clubs, pubs – a vibrant place.
But unchanged haven –- just in case.

One more summer and then – it's
their home no longer.

Years pass – what's this?
Children's children fill our space.

So much the same – and yet . . .

Celia Andrews

The Valley Of Sin/Happy Valley

I live in the valley between Soden and Gomorrah,
Where no one seems to care if the world ends tomorrow.
They have forgotten about Jesus who died on a tree
Only thinking of self and debauchery
They care not for those that in need
And care only for pleasure and their own greed
I have been tempted to do wrong
But the Lord my God bid me to be strong
To turn my back on all wicked ways
And to follow him all of my days
People mock and make fun of me
But they are blind and cannot see
How life on Earth is meant to be
Must I stand by and watch this wicked sin?
With a torment that rages from deep within
Or have I the courage to stand and fight?
And proclaim Jesus with all my might
Will they listen? Who can tell
For in this valley many sinners dwell!

Jean Ruth

Just Flying Rats

I wasn't usually out at night, thought the dark would be a cover.

'Where you goin' wi' that ladder, dick'ead?' 'Perving?' 'Perving on little kids?'

The crescendo to this symphonic abuse, the first punch, I don't remember feeling. Up above the circle of attackers, out of my body, I watched the blows rain in, kick, punch, me lying over the ladder, secateurs on the floor I hadn't thought to use.

****

They'd renovated the tunnel, made it a one-way taxi rank, upgraded the lighting. Then it began: the green netting pinned across the girders.

The pigeons, who nested in the girders, were displaced as the pinning progressed, squeezed from their nests like toothpaste from a tube. After a couple of weeks, it was complete.

The next day, I noticed a pair of pigeons, perched on the last girder. Later, as I walked back through, I saw why the pair remained: their chick was trapped on upside of the netting.

****

My hospital stay was mercifully short, returning to work on the sixth day.

I saw the pair straight away. Amazed, I pictured myself, discarded crutches, climbing the ladder and cutting the netting, freeing the chick, just as planned.

Then I saw, draped on the netting, like a sock over a washing line, the chick. I wasn't sure if the pair knew what death was, so they stayed, uncertain what to do, or, rather, if it was the defiance of their love.

I had failed love.

Ben Spencer

Lord We Don't Know Why

Lord we don't know why
Things happen as they do
You have your plans
We need to simply trust you
For everything is in your hands
And every child, woman and man
God of all creation
Be with us day by day
To acknowledge you
And to always pray
We know we fail you sometimes
In the things we think, say and do
We ask for your forgiveness
But also your blessings too
Help us to obedient
And listen only to your voice
To try to do what is always right
And make the right choice
We know you love us all
For you are a god of love
Help us to keep on the right path
Oh sovereign Lord above
For we are weak and sometimes fall
Give us your divine guidance
So we can stand tall
When our time is through dear Lord
May we have stood the test
For then we know we have our
Home in heaven
And eternal rest.

Barbara Miller

Heartlines

To: with my compliments. Please indicate which particular piece(s) you would like inserted in 'Heartlines'.

Dour, hard drinking, puritanical Scots male seeks 18-year-old bimbo to solace him in retirement to isolated Hebrides Croft. Those with silicone boobs need not apply.

'Born Again Robbie Burns' seeks 'not so gentle Mary' to share copious wee drams and duels with dirks 'Down in the Glen' – Glencoe, that is!

Braw, toothless Glaswegian laddie, battle (bottle) scarred and bitten, seeks tuneful, tawdry tart for duet menacing rendition of 'Of Flower of Scotland' at Hawick Women's Institute. Only Harridans need apply.

Surly, savage Scot – (descendant of the Earl of Bothwell) seeks reincarnated Mary Queen of Scots for persistent plotting in the bowels of Glamis Castle. Must be prepared to meet the legendary ***monster!***

Cocky Jock with impressive Claymore yearns for Maura Anderson clone to partner him in the 'Dashing White Sergeant' at the expatriate Scots Christmas soiree. Dress – Kilts ***(no knickers!)***

Kilted Scottish soldier with splendid sporran seeks spirited female with fiery bush to fight and imbibe with him in bleak Shetland Croft, (Mid Yell). Amenities include well maintained graveyard, one post office giving the names of the nearest Alcoholic Resource Centres.

Black-hearted Scot – keen collector of dead Sassenachs teeth (extracted at the Battle of Bannockburn) needs three more molars to complete tasteful table decoration to grace his dinner table for Hogmanay.

'Lady from Hell' Hun-hater – lonely, argumentative and anti-social, wishes to meet voluptuous Virago for tempestuous tussles in the trenches. Applicants must be worthy with fierce personality and able to demonstrate the blood-curdling battle cry employed by the Highlanders at the Battle of Culloden and other such battles.

Sentimental Scot with yen to warble 'Scotland the Brave' on traffic island sited in the middle of Sauchiehall Street, Glasgow, seeks *Scottish* soprano to provide descant. Perks include kilt-groping, Sassenach slagging, acrimonious rows and door-slamming during 'at home rehearsals'. No faint hearts please!

Lustful, lowland laddie yearns for 'Jean Brodie in her prime' for unstinting creme de la creme lechery behind the blackboard. Noto Bene: Proud owner of formidable fencing foil.

Kenneth McKellar – hoarse from many renditions of 'The Road to the Isles' desires to meet tolerant trollop who will turn a blind eye to his frequent gargling with 'Teachers' TCP and be winsome and wanton beneath the ***plaid!***

Andy Stewart double – addicted to haggis and fine malt whiskey wishes to offer false bonhomie, heart and Dirk of Steel in Velvet Sheath in maudelin homage to feisty female.

Argumentative Celt male wishes to meet soulmate for vitriolic verbal sparring and parsimony to share joint reclusion in wind-lashed Orkney Croft and to assist him in maintaining Still. Would suit sturdy strumpet. Plenty of bed and liquid breakfast. Porridge if desired.

Patsy McLean

The Bell

I was thinking of life and everything and heaven and hell
and then I heard the bell
honouring the moment
with its sonorous celebration.

I was thinking of paradox and the contradictions of fate
I was thinking of my bad luck of late
I was thinking of war and love and hate
I was thinking of the interest rate
I was thinking of the world and its appalling state
and will I have enough food on my plate
and will I reach the pearly gates
and then I heard the bell
honouring the moment
the here
the now
the past is gone it seemed to say
the future will have to wait.

Gary Austin

Chateauneuf Du Papageno

Papageno began juggling at a travelling circus
Bright red neon lights flashed: 'The Secret of Life is Here'
The twinkle in Burkhard's eye, won the hearts of all of us
The opera began, with a fun and magical atmosphere.

O blithe 'Papa' I have heard, I hear thee and rejoice,
Papageno, shall I call thee 'Bird', or but a wandering voice.

Sir Thomas Allen had a different role in this Magic Flute,
With him in the role of director we were so impressed
Kit Hesketh-Harvey as librettist we must salute:
With his adlibs, quips and jokes, he was simply 'the best'.

O blithe 'Papa' I have heard, I hear thee and rejoice,
Papageno, shall I call thee 'Bird', or but a wandering voice.

Pamina was beautifully sung by lovely Laura Mitchell
Nicky Spence, a great Tamino: the best diction ever,
Miners and nuns both formed part of the joyous carousel
Bird flu our Papageno – made him 'under the weather'.

O blithe 'Papa' I have heard, I hear thee and rejoice,
Papageno, shall I call thee 'Bird', or but a wandering voice.

The fuming red-eyed serpent was like the War Horse puppet
The three boys and their brollies, resembled Mary Poppins
Animal umbrellas, flying birds and hookas: all part of the great set
Papageno echoed Scotland's 'just say no' to drugs: stick to vitamins!

O blithe 'Papa' I have heard, I hear thee and rejoice,
Papageno, shall I call thee 'Bird', or but a wandering voice.

The music and magic of Mozart's opera are quite miraculous
As we wander through the temples – of nature, wisdom and reason
Searching for enlightenment and virtue to bless us
Is such joy, as all ends in both love and emancipation.

O blithe 'Papa' I have heard, I hear thee and rejoice,
Papageno, shall I call thee 'Bird', or but a wandering voice.

The little Pappagenis were pushed in prams by their many nurses
For this 'The Holiness of Great Light' – the lighting was a sensation
Where's Tamino's Scottish accent – that would take too many verses
Chateauxneuf du ***what?*** Help – we may need detoxification.

Mary Robertson

Trees

Trees – tall, beautiful,
Standing strong,
I stand and look at you hard and long,
Thinking of time long gone
Of all you've seen and all you have done.

Like sheltering people from the wind,
The rain and the sun,
Over hundreds of years
Since your life begun.

The changes in 'time'
How the world has changed,
From Penny Farthing bikes and little trikes.
The horse and carriage and the carts as well,
All trundling to markets over the dell.

What wonderful stories to us you could tell

Autumn comes – your leaves start to fall – and that's not all,
Along comes winter – your branches now bare
From the wind and the snow,
Just leave you standing there.
You look beautiful with the snow around and settled on the ground.

Spring now comes – you are beautiful still,
Leaves appearing on your branches to fill,
Birds will build nests where the sun will rest.

So many stories you have – to tell,
But I will stand and wonder,
My imagination to dwell.

Your strength give to others
As we stand 'neath your leaves,
Our backs leaning for strength
As you touch the backs of our knees.

Summer is here – you are in all your glory
As some of you have blossom
Another story.

Shirley Monaco

His Memory Lives On

The young lad left home as he heard his mother cry
For how long they said their goodbye
For the queen and country he was going to serve
A brave face it took plus a great deal of nerve
To countries afar he was sent
No hotels just a tent
Friends he made and friends he lost
His whole career came with a cost
Weeks to months and months to years
Many a laugh and many a tear
A lonely grave in a lonely place
But a smile his mother will remember on his lovely face.

Diane Young

Another Breath Of Spring

Come, come with me, to my space yet once again
Tiny shafts of yellow brighten the gloom
Fish jump expectantly they too feel the hope
Hope that comes with new dawning
Mellow calendines cup their blooms
With pale golden wonder
Flower buds on trees like tiny white pebbles
Waiting to burst into feathery blooms
The air is soft, and bird calls trill through
Newly cut grass dispels sweetness, when trodden on
My faithful friend with feet in the air, rolls with glee
Do you need inviting to my special space,
Or do you have your own secluded paradise?

Joan Skinner

Squeeze

Two sets of five toes were thrust into shoes
Though they objected, it was of no use.
Maybe elegant, straight as an arrow –
But both feet knew at once – far too narrow.
How did their person expect to get by
Teetering on heels so insanely high?

That person knew they did not feel at ease,
That person did not care about the squeeze.
Inside a car, discomfort not too bad
But window shopping, the mood-swing not glad.
Increased pressure was irking our twosome,
Inhabiting such shoes, more than gruesome.

One of the Big Toes started to complain,
'When will our our Toes find freedom again?
Surely our person has enough grey cells
To understand what our torment foretells?
What else but that person's own misery?'

The other Big Toe was heard to mutter,
'Our heel caught a kerb. Oops! Here's the gutter.
At least one foot is liberated now.
Fraternal Big Toe, lose your shoe somehow.
Both our feet must feel no more strain or stress,
And no future squeeze cause so much distress.'

Chris Creedon

Corfu

The plane was full
So was I –
Of thoughts that didn't matter
I felt it pull me to the sky
Thank God I wasn't fatter

No room to stretch
My rugby legs
I could not close my eyes
The book I'd read
On building regs
Had cut me down to size

And there was Venice
Down below
I'm blowed if I could see!
I took the pilot's word for it
And clutched my duty free!

We skimmed the waves
Just like a game I played
Of ducks and drakes
And when we hit the runway
Was I glad the plane had brakes

The taxi sped from Corfu Town
I hardly saw the route
Overtaking on the bends
With just a friendly toot
At last the villa!
And so dispensed with
All preliminaries
I can feed upon the sun
And plates of calamares!

Paul Gabriel

Faded But Not Forgotten

In my mind's eye I hear the sound
Of gunfire, a god's voice booming out,
Painting crimson stains
upon the muddy trenches
Saturating the already
Death-stale ground.
Fallen fragile bodies
Locked in eternal youth,
So many brave soldiers
Erased before their time,
Pulled within the reaper's embrace
They now lay still like statues
Staring sightlessly
Up at the silent sky,
Cut off in mid stride
Their screams echoing out
Long after they have gone on
Into death's dark shade.
So many taken . . .
Now only memories remain,
Photo albums flicked through
As families trace lovingly
The faces of their
lost brothers, sons,
Husbands and fathers.
Faded but not forgotten
History carves their names
Into its pages,
To remind all those who come after
How so many gave up so much
For a future they would never be a part of
For a dream of peace that will one day finally come to pass.

Melissa Wild

My World, My Village

Definition of a village that one will see
Is human occupation or community
Houses of all shapes and sizes
Ancient and modern as time devises
From generation to generation
Families made a living and a home
The place they return to
Wherever they roam
In my lifetime I have lived in three
Each with its own character to see
The one I lived in longest is the best that it can be
It has moved so far in the twentieth and twenty-first century
The landscape has changed slightly with lots of modern things
The extra buildings that fill the views which once were free
So a different perspective is what you see
The footpaths and the fields we could walk through
Have not altered in any way
Always used for years and a day
The flora and the fauna has been preserved
By order of conservation keeping the wild vegetation
More trees have been planted areas made good
Even planted a whole new wood
But in the living village the folks who reside
Living their lives as lifestyle decrees
The pattern of life whatever it be
Work or social whatever the occasion
Each joining in their own occupation
The church and the chapel village hall and school
All help to teach and learn life's rules
The church bells chime
The church clock tells the time
The village hall is where all sorts meet
The school gives much pleasure in so many ways
Not just to the children but folks of any age
A picturesque walk down an old Roman road
Takes one's thoughts and memories to days of old
When battles were fought and victories won
From all pages of history we shall never know
Who walked before us and where did they go?

The stream winding its way along its course
Another world within the water
Curious children love to fish and explore
Or anyone can watch from the bank to see
What secrets are there from you and me
So as we live each day and do our part
To help to keep the village going for the next generation
The village I live in is my world . . .

Marie Spanton

The Muse Of Mermaids – An Extract

Chapter 1: Angelo's Odyssey

Angelo Silvano's boat had not appeared in the marina for several months. However Helena knew intuitively he was making his way back to her. She had a clear image in one of her lucid dreams of Angelo, at the helm of the vessel that was symbolic of his freedom. The sea wind was in his long, dark hair, blown away from his face, and his mouth smiling, illuminating his features which were always too serious and brooding whenever he had to remain still or on land for too long.

Three days later after this dream Helena was not surprised to see Angelo's boat called Calypso, moored in the marina while she walked her pharaoh hound named Anubis, one morning before going to work. The boat's name of Calypso along with the eye of Osiris, said in Mediterranean legends to ward off evil spirits at sea had been freshly painted by Angelo. The letters of Calypso were black on a clean white background uncomplicated and plain unlike her captain.

Helena decided to return to Calypso and Angelo later as looking at the watch that he had given her for her last birthday, it was barely nine of the clock in the morning. Helena's soul belonged to a different age, certainly not in keeping with a digital one, and early morning wake up calls were not to Angelo's liking. Helena loved Angelo deeply but she was never prepared to tolerate his mercurial temperament and had made him aware of this on their last meeting six months ago...

Yazmin White

This Beautiful Place

No high mountains,
Or sand and sea,
But still there's much
To pleasure me.

Roman armies
Trod my county,
Searching for the
Richest bounty.

There's an abbey,
Built on a hill,
With Roman bricks
That linger still.

Lovely buildings,
Centuries old,
In St Albans,
I'm truly sold.

Old water mills,
Still grinding flour,
A happy place
To spend an hour.

Some fine houses,
And gardens too,
Fun to explore
And wander through.

The bluebell woods
Are such delight,
A springtime treat
For nose and sight.

Ashridge forest,
Where live the deer,
If I'm lucky
I get quite near.

Hills and valleys,
Where chalk streams flow,
These are places
I like to go.

It's nice to live
In Hertfordshire,
Where loveliness
Is always near.

Hazel Cullis

When I'm Tired

When I'm tired,
Stressed,
A little depressed,

Close your eyes,
Guide me through,
But don't speak,

Let the wind whisper,
Your words of relief,
Don't leave me in the deep,

Hold my hand,
Out of the gutter,
Other stand by,

I can feel you pull,
The earth shakes,
Objects scatter,

Things crumble, disintegrate,
Before life falls,
Back into place.

Kirsty Elizabeth Naylor

The Extravagant Stranger

Defying all boundaries, defying all danger,
Every day's an adventure for the 'extravagant stranger'.
Too foreign for home, too foreign for abroad
But he's strong and determined, he beats the odds.
The extravagant stranger turns turf to treasure
They're jealous of him, but he never bows to pressure
Too tired from battle but too strong to quit
He's doing it for tomorrow's sake, his dream is legit
For the extravagant stranger, friends are luxurious
He doesn't get too attached, all ends are spurious
Constantly alert while awake and while half dead
Charged by ambition, fuelled from dreams in his head.
The extravagant stranger finally finds a land
He toils it and creates an oasis from what was sand
He grows an orchard and he shares his fruit
But now they reject him and tell him to find his roots
It doesn't matter that he was a game-changer
He endangers and will always be an extravagant stranger.

Toks Hussain

By The Kitchen Door

It's a sure peculiarity of English weather
that yesterday, as I rambled this track,
the rain spiked my face

and weighted my coat – today
only the dulled bank of moping nettles
give testament

to the swollen river, and on the flagstone,
the pair of sodden walking boots
still struggling to dry.

Ben C Clark

Faith

For the breath that stained the glass, alas.
Long centuries now are done and past.
But chanting, be-robed the tangent goes on,
As an archipelago of acolytes,
Hard faced and grim, with eyes of flint
Stalk superstition's shivering haunts.
From the beauty of the whitest dove
These tawdry hawks, shaped lovingly,
March four-square forwards, arm in arm,
Death snarling out of beauty's breast,
Goose-stepping down the bones of time,
Through supplication's history,
Jack-booted choreography
To trample through those eyes of ash
There coldly staring heavenly,
At that juggernaut of certainty.

And the breath that stained the glass, alas,
Still frozen by the wint'ry blast,
Becomes sharp, shattered, jagged spells
Which cut and sear ten billion times.
'Til, through the broken, misted glass
Wiped by the human sleeve,
The siren superstition still slyly smiles her smile.

David Jones

Just My Luck

It was just my luck not to see your heart
As fate would have it we lived miles apart
Years passed and then came the day
I boarded the train and you were on your way
The date was set and we arranged to meet
My heart began skipping a beat

There you were tall and proud
Waiting for me at the train station
From the window I wanted to shout aloud
And hug you with much adoration
I stepped out and you enveloped me in your arms
And I felt your love upon me
Oh, how I missed being captivated by your charms
And how you smiled so sweetly

Here we were now facing each other
Our eyes gazing and longing to love
You said to me, 'Now we're together'
I then replied, 'Thank heavens above'
I could never envision a day
On how I would pave a life of my own
Just my luck I have you today
And grateful I am not alone

Months have passed with time lost in ether
Our lives seem to stop and start
We spend a little time having a laugh together
But then we get torn apart
A wish for us to pack up and get away
Just the two of us to fall in love
Has never arisen on any day or holiday
And we have nothing to speak of

How does one keep love for another
When they say you do not belong
Or never see you as a future partner
So that it pierces the heart so strong?
It was just my luck not to feel love from you
For that is how my destiny came to be
Through the looking glass with no romantic view
I now lay down lifeless, resting peacefully

Anoushka Sharma

A Slave To Life

A slave to life, from the day we are born
As we ride the waves of an unpredictable storm
Our mortal spans, of miniature seconds is the time
Survive the strokes of moments in line
As the eternal clock rolls on
Eons have been and gone
No beginning and no end
As the finger points on an ever turning bend
Each second, each hour, each day
Too large the time to comprehend that way
And yet, we live in our minute allotted space
On the ticking course in the constant race
When our time has come
Life, expelled and done
Do we start all over again?
Rebirth in another life, do we regain
Tick tock goes the life as if taking stock
As a heart beats as ticking clock
We leave behind our spent remains
And the mere pang of mortal pains

Terry Powell

Knight Of Aragon

Spoken word

The Templar of Aragon was summoned to avenge all wrongdoers,
And on a white cloud of memories; he rode through the gates of yesterday.
His steed, a cold black unicorn, carried him on his journey,
That would be long, and full of darkness.
Yet, filled with hope for a pure future.

Sing

He is the knight of Aragon
Here for all to see.
He is the knight of Aragon
Here to set you free.

Spoken word

In his silence, he gathered the comets of the universe,
To give him the symbol, to destroy the pathway of evil.
The pilgrim of the future passed over this Earth;
And with a wave of his sword of justice;
Began the destruction of the sinister, mystical darkness.

Sing

He is the knight of Aragon
Here for all to see.
He is the Pilgrim of the Light
Here to set you free.

Sing

Amidst the flames and the cries, of men who were dying,
The wind of a tempest, was felt everywhere.
A scourge on the Earth, became a nemesis,
Casting the darkness back to its lair.
See the knight of Aragon, here to set you free,
He is the Pilgrim of the Light, to change the world to be.

Spoken word

After seven weary days, of drawing down the jackals of retribution,
The gods decreed that halcyon would descend over these lands.

And in a small hamlet; a newborn child, filled the night air with its crying;
indicating to the pilgrim; that rejuvenation was returning.

Sing

He is the knight of Aragon
Here for all to see.
He is the knight of Aragon
Here to set you free.

Spoken word

At length, the pilgrim drew his mantle over the scorched wastelands,
Although the stench of death was still prevalent.
The four riders of the apocalypse, had retreated, from whence they came,
And a gentle breeze swathed the world with a composed serenity.

Spoken word

His sword now pointed to the stars of the night sky, and they aligned themselves, for a story yet to be told.
The moonlight glistened, and the horizon highlighted, by the aurora borealis;
But from these archaic ruins, and a new found freedom;
Would grow the tranquillity and beauty, for our future world.

Sing

He is the knight of Aragon
Here for all to see.
He is the Pilgrim of the Light
Here to set you free.
The Pilgrim of our freedom
And the world to be.

R Barnett

Over The Top

The whistle blows,
Final for some,
And the men mount
Ladders out of
Trampled trenches;
As to the gallows,
Silently pleading
For reprieve

An officer leads
Brandishing a revolver,
Out of range of the enemy
And good only
For the encouragement
Of stragglers,
Momentarily sceptical
About the grand plan

The Germans had swapped
Industrial efficiency
For chivalry,
And aligned their Maxims
In the optimum X-formation;
So that the spinning
Eviscerating rounds
Never missed

Men fall,
Muscle and soft tissue pulped;
Air gulped,
Remonstrating
For the torn man's tipple
Of lukewarm water
From a khaki canteen

At last
An officer minds
The Balaclava mindset;
And signals the retreat
To the waterlogged trench:
Survivors shiver
At the thought
Of the next sortie

David Burl

Words . . .

Pour smooth as honey from my hive-like mind
In fresh flowered, deep, desultory dreams,
Congeal on virgin-white paper to find
Conflicting emotions' divulging streams,
Which pass beneath shadows of solitude,
Where faltering hopes fade to foggy night:
In wisdom's grace the muses now exude –
Bright beams of inspirational respite.
When there's no human contact, words are friends
Who do not judge, or try to quench my fire,
And each well-chosen sentence comprehends
An outpouring of linguistic desire.

Distant city lights fade beyond the room,
In quiet hours my flowing thoughts resume.

David Norris-Kay

The Place My Heart Lies

I imagine the place
high on the crest of a wave.

Birds float, riding reins of galloping tides
and sea spray clouds that envelop rock and stone.
Attacked and embraced
an enemy faced
eternally battered by ocean lines
but steadfast and still in salty battles.

In calmer breezes, waves lap toes of majestic giants
magnificent stony-faced guardians
protectors of the soft flesh
of England's torso.

The ocean in submission, retreating.

My heart lies high on the dappled face,
cooling itself in rapid winds
forgetting itself in sea-blue dreams
its home in the spoils of a battle won
on a cliff's high shoulder,
proud and at peace.

Lisa Winship

The Banshee

My bed is a floating island
Upon a hot teal sea.
The Underworld lurks beneath
And at my window, a banshee.

The raindrops are her claws
Scratching at the glass.
Wind and thunder are her voice
Of a thousand souls that passed.

With her serpent's tongue
She whips the trees,
And floating down in loss of life
Are the silhouettes of dying leaves.

The banshee rattles the windowpanes
And beckons to be let in.
A fork of lightning strikes her head
The banshee shall not win.

Her skin secretes a sulphuric stench
Which tickles her own nose.
Outside it is silent, her storm has died
And in yellow smoke, she goes.

Lizza Lane

A Letter To The Prime Minister

Dear Mr Prime Minister,
a recent article in The Mail
claimed that there are now more
chickens in the world than humans.

We must move to cap such an
influx of poultry immediately.
After all, Hitchcock did warn us.

I see those hens, parading their
tail feathers, like trollops,
for the sake of the cock.

And he, himself a vain pervert,
selects the younger ones for
such a lewd parody of matrimony.

He then will have the audacity
to wake us up early,
it really is a pattern of behaviour
that many of us cannot tolerate.

I'd really like to know what
you are planning
to dispose of such a menace.
Yours faithful
A Bigert.

Stephen Foot

Death's Open Door

In this dark and forlorn room, stirring impish thoughts to bloom,
unnatural thoughts should not be said, lest it should fall upon your head.

Where candlelight creates its own with shadows stalking, freely roam.
Waltzing off into the night with dancing flame at merest slight.

Following, guiding, leading way. Silhouette in constant play
from darkest corner of the room, shimmering light does start to bloom.

The palest hint of glowing red appearing at the foot of bed.
A single spark though barely warm, expands with linking, swathing swarm.

Enveloping before my very eyes, this mass extrudes to mortal guise,
suspended upright gathering dense of human form with no pretence.

Instructing me with single hand, is gesture, no, in fact demand,
of that concourse I am most sure as finger motion makes its lure.

With fear aligned upon my face and beating heart my blood does race,
two drying lips with palate sour that quiver like some windswept flower.

I have no wrap to screen this tense mauling from the elements,
I flounder forward so demure, this life before me, insecure.

At whose command I have no reign my reservations cry in vain,
with unheard screams that I bestow, cast on candlelight's shadow.

Whistling off into the night as I am drawn to scheduled plight.
Barefoot we walk along the shore, confronted by death's open door.

Retrieving now that one last look as final breath is rankly took,
I cast my eyes upon the bed, external shell, so pale, so dead.

I turn around to welcome host, he that of light, me that of ghost,
I follow him into that place, where one can look up on his face.

My life, expired, showed good intent a time I feel was worthwhile spent
and following happily through the haze such sights I see do so amaze.

If I had words what would they be that could express the joys I see?
Cry not for me, try not to mourn this soul of mine has been reborn.

Christopher Bayliss

The First Gulf War

Two oil wells on a border line.
An argument that's left for a time,
The United Nations turning its back,
On the claims of Iraq.
An invasion that lasted an hour,
United Nations left to look and glower,
Resolutions hurried through,
Taking nine hundred oil wells just won't do!

He's gassed the Kurds, five thousand of them,
He's no regard for the lives of men.
He's killing Kuwaitis just for fun,
Something's definitely got to be done!
I don't like it any more than you
So we'll have a war, a just one too!
We'll launch the might of thirty nations
Against this man with ideas above his station,
And twenty-nine others just like we,
Believe Kuwaitis must be free.

And so they launched a six week attack
On major cities in Iraq.
Oil and gas and power station
And all that made the Iraqi nation
Were bombed strategically, it was said,
To leave the minimum civilian dead,
Because the UN had gone to war,
Against Saddam not the country's poor.
So every advance that the country had made,
Was completely destroyed in a six week air raid.

With nothing left in the cities to hit,
'Better start on the army,' Bush had to admit.
Send in the boys with their tanks and their gun
We'll soon have the Iraqis on the run.
Better make the boys feel at home to boot,
We'll cut them off and kill them in a turkey shoot.

And of course there is no better way,
To see our weaponry on display.
Poor Iraqis have got no chance,
We knew that six months in advance.
And so the generals gave the order,
For that hundred thousand man Iraqi slaughter.

One hundred hours later, the world war won,
The feeling of a job well done.
The hoisting of the Kuwaiti flag,
Makes presidents of the thirty brag.
The smoke from oil wells now on fire
The rain clouds turned as black as mire.
Not much money in Kuwaiti coffers,
America accepting reconstruction offers.
Bush tells Iraqis to go on the attack,
'Get rid of Saddam,' but he fights right back.
Shiite and Kurd left to bear the brunt
Of taking part in Bush's Saddam Hussein witch hunt.

Peter Edwards

The Princess

She wakes. And from her fitful sleep
she rises and in her fancy's play,
she looks out from her castle keep
and dreams of freedom far away.

The rising stars shine bright and clear.
She kneels to face the valued skies
and captured in each crystal tear,
the heavens glisten in her eyes.

In supplication to the spheres;
the arbiters of destiny,
she begs an answer to her prayers;
an end to her captivity.

And now the stars give their assent
and bind a champion to her case.
A bolt across the firmament
proclaims his mark – and marks his place.

But subtle are the ways of fate.
Its twisted thread perversely flows;
whose bounty often soon or late
brings blessings bound to greater woes.

Upon her lyre she plays an air
that echoes from its golden strings.
Her song is like a sacred player.
The angels listen as she sings.

Across the lake that girdles round
the tower where she's languished long,
two brothers slumber on the ground
in earshot of her plaintiff song.

Their livery is red and white –
red thunderbolts on argent fields,
with spurs that sparkle in the light
and silver bosses on their shields.

As if by nature one is broken
and made up into two the same;
their faces bear the self-same token.
Their only difference is a name.

One, roused, by the celestial fire,
which sparks across the lucid night
now stirs to hear her raptured lyre
and gazes on her window's light.

A vision in the moonlight there,
she gleams upon the crystal water.
The starlight glistens in her hair;
as though she were a fairy's daughter.

He sees, and wants her for his own,
and reckless now in his desire,
He scales the dizzy heights of stone;
each lofty crag, each and thrusting spire.

But fate then spins its iron loom
and weaves its web of baleful weft;
to cast the threads which bind their doom
in grief and death and love bereft.

Enchanted by each other's face,
their hearts and bodies soon engage
and on her bed of silk and lace
they touch, they kiss, their passions rage.

But now he must fulfil the vow
made at his father's dying breath;
their enemy, to overthrow;
return in victory or death.

They kiss and so they bid farewell,
but as he leaves he gives his word
to free her from her lofty cell,
by grace, or favour, or the sword!

So slowly pass the hours' flight,
through days and nights to his return.
She watches from her topless height.
She watches whilst the candles burn.

At last she sees the people come,
with knight and page and seneschal.
He seems to bring the laurel home,
to ride in triumph joined by all!

But sombre drums beat deep and slow.
A chequered knight lies on a bier.
The heralds hang their standards low.
His crimson thunderbolts are clear.

These are his marks she knows full well,
and reels beneath this bitter blow;
but does not know and cannot tell
it is his brother, there below.

Beset by grief her reason fails.
Cursing the bitter jests of Fate;
upon the parapet she wails,
and plunges headlong by the gate.

Dismayed, the folk before the towers,
look down upon her broken frame;
where; from a bed of broken flowers,
her lifeless eyes stare up in blame.

And so the people bear her up
then set a cross upon her breast
by sacred book and sacred cup
within the chapel's place of rest.

But as they kneel to say a prayer,
a warhorse thunders from afar.
A knight rides up with arms aflare
and helmet gleaming like a star.

His helm is decked with garland leaf
and thunderbolts adorn his shield.
The tidings of his brother's death
have pressed him hotly from the field.

They look upon his blazoned crest.
They look once more upon the slain
and cross themselves in terror, lest
the walking dead ride forth again.

He rips his harness clear away;
the book is rent, the chalice flies,
his sable locks have turned to grey
and madness echoes in his cries.

He lifts the garland from his brow
and so adorns his brother's head,
then gently rocks her to and fro,
and lifts her from her sacred bed.

And there along the waterside;
a meadow where the sweet birds sing,
he makes her grave, and lays inside
the fragrant flowers of the spring.

The waters there are cold and still
They beckon him to enter deep.
He enters in to drink his fill
of darkness and eternal sleep.

And now beside the ancient wood
their bones decay in silent gloom.
But when the moon is in its flood
their shades forsake the earthly tomb.

For mortals slain by their own hand
do penance long beyond the grave.
Their spirits wake to walk the land;
The wood, the meadow and the cave.

And so she chants a death lament
and from the shadows bids him rise.
Then from the deeps his shade is sent
with tears of longing in his eyes.

He walks across the living water;
she treads the air beneath her feet.
In silent words and silent laughter,
the insubstantial lovers meet.

Embracing by the margin's edge
they drift into the starlit glade,
and make once more their lovers' pledge'
until the stars and moonbeams fade.

They pass the glade and cross the meadow,
to wander from her loamy cell
and walk the realms of dreaming shadow
where living souls may never dwell.

So many moons, so many morrows,
so many vows they still must face,
before they leave this place of sorrows;
set free from this accursed place.

But glad to serve their days unnumbered;
they linger in their dark domains;
for when at last their curse is sundered
they'll join in bliss on Heaven's plains.

Steve Waterfield

Septic Tank

What secret shame did I cause you,
To be so unceremoniously dumped,
Like bodily waste, in a cesspit?
What moment of careless passion would I have laid bare
For all and sundry to see and to sneer and disown you?
Did I not even merit some memorial,
Other than that now etched forever on your haunted soul?
What perverse morality let you dismiss my death
As deliverance, a merciful relief?

Is there no love, no empathy, no redemption,
To heal this brokenness done in distressed confusion?
And what of God, so central to your culture and life?
Did he condone this heartless whitewash, or turn a blind eye,
Or did He not weep through the bleeding heart of His Son,
Who also was disowned and broken?

Stephen Watson

What's Going On?

Why are the kerbs so much higher now?
Why are the roads much longer?
Why does everyone mumble so?
Why are my spectacles stronger?

My family say that I shout down the phone
That I turn up the telly too high.
But if everyone spoke with clearer precision
I'd hear what they say – wouldn't I?

There's so much bad temper upon the roads
Where everyone makes such a fuss.
I drive my car slowly, ignoring the chaos.
Why should I be using the bus?

Why are clothes labelled wrongly today?
I now have to wear an eighteen.
My usual size hardly covers my thighs
And my stomach folds look quite obscene.

The makers of screw-top bottles and jars
Design lids that are stuck on too tight.
My grip always slips and nothing will move
As I struggle with all of my might.

As for lipstick! What rubbish they offer us now
It spreads up my lips like a spider.
I waste money on creams that do no good at all
And my wrinkles get wider and wider.

I can't digest food. What do they put in it?
I have to leave half on my plate.
I used to drink beer but one pint is my limit.
So why am I putting on weight?

The world is becoming strange and unfair,
Everything's turning around.
I'm losing my memory, losing my hair,
And soon I'll be under the ground.

Philippa Bower

Unscattered

With both hands on the steering wheel
Leant forwards with his head between
He takes a last long lasting breath
Emits a cough to clear his chest
He checks his watch against the clock
He then secures the steering lock
Folds up his Lakeland fishing mag
Picks up his ragged duffle bag
He locks the car and checks the handle
Checks the tyres from every angle
Then walks the car park long way round
Roots in his pocket for a pound
And in the foyer drops it in
The British Heart Foundation tin
He pats the ragged duffle bag

He browses tools he owns already
Browses ornamental teddies
He watches on a twelve inch screen
A demonstration, how to clean
Your gutters with some new device
He picks one up and thinking twice
He puts it back and moves along
He watches parakeets in song
Observes a hamster in its wheel
He browses farm-house ready meals
He looks at books and DVDs
He looks at small leylandii trees
He looks at bulbs and bedding plants
He looks at socks and underpants
And pats the ragged duffle bag

He shines an apple on his knee
And stirs a stewing pot of tea
He folds a crease down in his paper
And tears a voucher out for later
He pretends he hasn't noticed when
The cashier walks around again
Before returning to her group
Who whisper as they dish up soup:
How many days now in a row

How long he sits before he goes
He imagines that they speculate
Consider he has lost his mate
Consider he's alone at night
He imagines they are right
He pats the ragged duffle bag

Gareth Roberts

Walking Inside The Wind

Inside, outside, close and flying
the wind lifts and spirals
across the high clearness
the upturned tilt and circle of the sky.
Cloud, pink tinted, warmed
and kindled grey to smoke
swirls within an envelope of blue.

And I am walking, where the path
sucks in and bends the light
trees lifted into forks
as the field sweeps down
to pools of spreading water.
Reed grass straight and tracking air
the curve of semi-solid earth . . .

And the wind echoes
to the slow clap clap of white spinning blades . . .
As sun and earth repel and pull
repel and slow the moves
of that old circle dance.

As sun warms air above and sends it
plunging into cold, rolling down
that deep, deep gradient of sound.
Blows earthward through my skin
Tosses me high
Stills my voice . . .
Small pawn on a giant breathing wheel.

Pat MacKenzie

Dumping Crisis Is Growing, Says UN

You'll find me in hiding in a Third World tip
I'm e-waste posing as re-usable goods
We're undetected unless you should sip
Local water laced by some hi-tech hoods

My claim to fame is in my construction
You'll never know what laid you low
The elements causing your torso's ruction
Only chemical analysis on body will show

Was it Cadmium ingested? That's not very nice
Leaching into the fresh water course
Disease once known as 'itai-itai' or Japanese rice
They fed it to livestock, now full of remorse

Perhaps Tantalum was another ingredient
Only allowed if government permit intact
Breathe that one in and lesions are bent
On opening up in your respiratory tract

Of course I do have another old favourite
Lead that's the fellow (he carries some weight)
Damage a nervous system? Try chewing a bit
As barefoot children do when nothing on plate

Now Cobalt is on offer as toxin cardiomyopathy
It's in the Canadian beer! Don't ask what for
Such a lovely blue pigment when used in jewellery
It's what German miners called the Goblin ore

Tin there's a real nasty in Triethyltin form
Organic tin substance from out of the mine
Eye skin irritations, liver damage the norm
Brain damage usual unless caught in time

Nickel was named after the dwarf planet Ceres
With flammability that emits toxic fumes
Also has a radioactive risk if you please
Allergy cured only in good hospital rooms

I do have some Antimony built at my heart
Stops me catching alight when I'm too hot
You can't destroy it, it's an intrinsic part
Dump in the food chain! That's where they get shot

Eighteen atomic numbers go to make my parts
But if you want a favourite and winner and by far
It's Quicksilver once swallowed gives fits and starts
Remember Alice's Mad Hatter? Yes Mercury's the star

Charles Keeble

Storm

The morning breaks like a heart
torn by the separation of night;
dark clouds on the horizon
rise above the sea
where birds try to flee
from the oncoming storm.

The northern wind calls with rage,
dragging the sea
to the shore for support,
gouging the coastline
as though a ravenous wolf
wild with hunger.

The sky spits light with forked tongues,
severe and deadly;
stabbing at the ferocious fountain
heaving beyond its bounds,
tossing barges to their death
with no mourners to pay their respect.

The endless northern breath
sings its song with the drums;
rumbling, booming,
cracking its whip at the water
that obeys without question;
a slave of the storm.

Ron Larter

First Longing Fulfilled

High and wind-swept hillside – a cool, darkening, evening –
He, standing; she sitting by him –
Both gazing at the hills surrounding them;
Hardly daring to seek each other's eyes . . .

Thought he:
'If you would but lift your sweet face upwards to me, I would kiss those gentle lips. Yet, for love of you, I cannot allow my eager finger to lift your little chin up to me . . .'

Thought she:
'And I know full-well how you long to kiss my cheek, my lips, my hair. I hardly dare. How can it be? – woman like me . . . Oh! – my heart breaks – so sweet for us to be alone – and yet, and yet, I want more. I would gladly lift my face up to yours – I feel your need, your urgency: it matches mine . . .'

No further thoughts transmitted between the two.

She looked up into his eyes: saw reflection of her own need.

A kiss was planted, indeed – and more, upon her mouth, her cheeks, her neck. Hands joined in the joyous seeking; all barriers down, now: love's work in fullest bloom.

And, spent and breathless, arms about each other, the night crept on, the silence deepened.

They parted on the wind-swept hill. He went his way, she went hers.

Many a meeting thus ensued, each deeper and more meaningful than the last.

Aye, but none compared with the almost unbearably tender sweet simplicity of that first hushed, hesitant surrender.

Dorinda MacDowell

Out Into The Cold

Staring out the window, not making a sound.
The world is buzzing around and around.

I see the children with their mothers close by
Trips to the school, the shops or just strolling by.

I watch the weather, I watch the world, I watch the postmen and post girls.
I see the clouds as they float up high, I see the sun in the sky.

The birds are flying and making their nests, the dogs chase the cats, and they never rest.
The world how so lovely, so bright and alive, but for me a scary place is outside.

I can't go out, so I stay in, this phobia I have is killing my skin.
My fear to go out, it holds me back and I fear I will never get back on track.

I wish I could step over the threshold so close but without any help I'll become a ghost.
My life is wilting into nothing at all and I continue to stare at the same four walls.

I require some help, I'm screaming inside; please help, please help I want to survive.
Is there anyone out there who can help me be strong, and hold my hand whilst I put my coat on.

A friendly smile, a hand to hold and I could overcome my phobia and go out into the cold.

Julie Gibbon

I Hope This Was Never Meant

The power of imagination trampled,
As we stare into TV sets.
Books are bought for their covers,
Put in their place and never read.
Life is seen through a periscope of screens,
The adventure few will feel.
Computers and their games pushed out,
What we once all knew as real.
Clothes were handcrafted to be durable,
Now they're mass produced both worn and torn,
Magazines were once edifying and classy,
They're now mediums of hardcore-soft-porn.
Conversations are ancient fables,
The muted beats of keyboards now reign.
Dinner tables are now dinner couches,
And the concept of eye-to-eye is now inane.
Our adventures are seen by the unsocial masses,
And scrolled over without care.
Our successes are met by silent jealousy,
Successes only family seem to share.
Breaking news is now monotonous,
And celebrity culture now the rage.
The long pilgrimage to Mecca means bingo,
Now only a bus stop away.
Those who deserve the status of legend,
Are reduced to this week's fad,
The plethora of our language has been crippled,
A concentration that is mad.
Innovative verve is a memory,
Replaced by the stigma of being wrong.
Emotions are labelled as a weakness,
Limited to that of emoticons.
Art and creativity has been discarded,
They plague intelligence and its mould,
Success is measured by zeros on a bonus,
Not by growth or common goal.
Life used to be about the journey,
But now it's a commute without a view.
Relationships had stability,

But now almost everything falls through.
Communities were a tight knit,
Now we don't know our neighbour's name.
Honesty was predetermined,
Now we're desperate to shift the blame.
Seeking help with our hardships,
Has been swallowed by solitude.
Manners were once of great importance;
Now replaced by attitude.
Where we were once together, united,
We've fallen victim to dissent.
Now I think and ask rhetoric questions,
Hoping all this was never meant.

William Hunter Howell

Looking

I walk around the garden,
At the end of the day,
Making sure everything,
Is safely away,
And when it is a dark and clear night,
I look to the sky to see a,
Wonderful sight,
Stars shining like diamonds,
In a stone and then you think,
Are we alone,
So many planets, so much space,
There may well be another race,
But that's in the future for the people to see,
But for now looking at the stars,
Is good enough for me.

Robert Hunt

That Other Robin Knox

That other Robin Knox was a sailor too,
Two boats and a punt and his wife formed the crew,
Sailed the shoreline of Polkerris from east to west,
Past the harbour wall when conditions were best.

All kitted up for every situation,
Winches, flares, short wave radio, satellite navigation,
More versatile than Robin the famous,
A deep sea diver, a big fisherman, totally fearless,
Soles of lemon and Dover, sea bass and crustaceans were his prey,
Circumnavigated Mevagissey once on a memorable day.

No fish worth his salt should have swum into that bay,
When he was at large on those millpond days,
And lobsters and crab were no foil for his pots,
For a ruthless assassin was that other Robin Knox,
And with nets and waders and oilskins he looked the part,
Some looked on with wonder but tourists took him to heart.

Suddenly there came to an end to all of his plundering in,
A freak hot summer saw a school of killer whale come lumbering in,
Disturbing that other Robin Knox,
Out past the sea wall attending to his pots.
The naval reserve was summoned to the scene,
With harpoon, guns and a cannon and a Polaris submarine.

That other Robin Knox was in the thick of it all,
Whale and blubber, harpoon, missile, gunshot and cannonball,
Now encircled by whales, he spotted a gap and tried to break free,
But them whales were having a whale of a time, and gave him no liberty,
Then an ill directed harpoon went spiralling up in the air,
Coming down like a meteorite, catching him aware,
He was harpooned to his wishbone, nailed to the mast,
Then it sliced open the deck and he and that boat were both sinking fast.

Nobody was sure where they finally came to rest,
The swell them whales created sent that boat into the wilderness,
Teams of divers went down but failed to find his final resting place,
That other Robin Knox had seemingly gone without trace,
Some folk placed a buoy in an area which they thought marked the spot,
As a monument to him in the shape of a giant lobster pot,
But one of those big south westerly winds didn't like ti too much,
Sent it across to Holland, where it's now a curious fascination for the Dutch.

So he went up to that ocean in the sky,
Where all good fishermen go,
Where edible fish abound,
And where whales never show,
Where the prevailing winds are a gentle breeze,
With limitless time to be spent on calmer seas,
No storms or gales or currents to have to outfox,
A heavenly incarnation for that other Robin Knox.

Bernard Smith

Waiting

Day after lonely day, upon the park bench, hunched and still,
In deep repose
And blind, he listens to the murmur of the rill
And no one knows
He was a soldier once, locked with his comrades in the heat of war,
Watching them fall.
Stunned by the madness, by the terror, by the gore,
Yet he stood tall
Until that final day saw fate exact its toll
His world grew dim.
They sent him home to her, broken, no longer whole.
She cared for him.

Sun warms his ageing bones; he drifts to dream,
Anticipates.
In churchyard's shade, beyond the pebbled stream,
His love awaits.

He lifts his head to face,
With sightless eyes
The hallowed resting place
Wherein she lies . . .

David Shaw

A Soldier Named Francis Turner In Flander's Field

(Dedicated To My Great Uncle, Francis Turner 1896-1918)

He sat on the bare, dusty soil, just a
short distance from the trenches. The bloodstained
patches from those dead and wounded, must have
confused and sickened him. 'I have retained
my life,' he whispered to himself as he
looked across to a body shot in
his back. Men, with stretchers appeared. 'Was he
my friend?' Frank asked. Nobody spoke; shock
waves; Frank was viewing his own body laid:
carried away, away in fog and smoke.

Suddenly, there was singing, those voices
drew in close beside him. 'We're here for you
Frank.' White cloud replaced the smoke. 'Your choices
were the best.' The grass now green, a soul so true.

Pearl Burdock

Our BBC

A classic institution,
Such hardy constitution,
Loved by all with passion.
It's inviting, exciting, enticing:
Seizing, teasing, pleasing:
Contriving, striving, thriving:
Calling, enthralling, installing:
Negotiating, placating, debating:
Captivating, evaluating, exasperating:
Binding, minding, finding
Every moment a success,
Perfection performed no less.

Alison Hodge

A Date To Remember

Jean had waited for Steve for an hour and now she was going home. She looked again at the postcard he'd left in reception, the last morning of their holiday. It definitely said 9/8/2013 outside Cardiff Castle at 12.15. She'd walked up and down outside the castle and then crossed the road and hovered in the Welsh gift shop until the assistants started to look at her suspiciously. What a fool she'd been, a middle-aged widow waiting for a man she'd met on holiday. On an impulse she'd booked a week's touring holiday in Portugal, the first holiday since her husband's death. She'd been nervous about taking this first step and more so when she found that most of her fellow travellers were couples. There was, however, one other solitary traveller and naturally they were seated next to one another. He seemed disinclined to talk but the ice was broken when the couple sitting opposite thought they were married. Over the following week they found they had a lot in common and although sad to be flying home whilst Steve was staying another week in Portugal, Jean was delighted to receive his card. He'd explained he hadn't asked her in person in case she wasn't interested and was too polite to refuse.

The following month Steve waited for Jean outside Cardiff Castle in vain. Suddenly he realised he'd lived too long in America and had written the date the American way and not 8/9/2013.

Pat McKenna

The Capsized World Of Mr Toad

The cap size fitted Mr Toad,
who wore it bold with with blazer striped
upon the poop-poop-deck of a river boat,
where he proudly took a noble stand
against the egregious accusation
that *he* was all at sea.

Robert Black

Normandy Landing – Memoria In Aeterna

Allied morale plummeted fast in 1940, after France fell,
As Germans occupied Western Europe, by Blitzkrieg-hell;
A second front in Western Europe seemed to be the panacea,
Thus collaborated Churchill and Eisenhower – now, or never!
And Operation 'Neptune' 6-6-1944, chosen for Normandy landings,
Largest seaborne invasion with greatest military backings:
Secrecy paramount, and security covering every aspect,
Amphibious landings – Omaha: Utah: Gold: Sword: Juno: – in prospect:
With supporting roles at sea, and air, by Armed Forces and civilians:
Of Allied countries, cum American, British and Canadians.
Hitler placed Rommel in command along the Atlantic-Wall,
With gun emplacements, mines, wooden stakes – the enemy to foil.
Under umbrella, 'Operation Bodyguard', allies conducted deception
Misleading Germans – of Calais being possible second attack location:
Guided by lunar phase/tides/day and time/ and weather, blending,
Operation 'Neptune' was launched on D-Day – the masterpiece of planning.
Bombing of Normandy began around midnight – sans retreat,
Minesweepers began clearing channels for the invasion fleet:
The Western Task Force included battleships Ramillies, Waspite and Roberts.
Victory in Normandy stemmed from several factors –
German preparations along the Atlantic-Wall were in tatters
This led to the restoration of the French Republic – fait accompli,
And contributed to an Allied victory in the war, eventually.
Bells toll in unison, in remembrance of this 70th anniversary
For the 'Flowers of Youth, and Aged' who perished on air, land and sea.
Dulce et decorum est pro patria mori.

Foreign words and phrases:

Memoriain aeterna (L) = In eternal remembrance
Blitzkrieg (G) = Lightning war
Fait accompli (Fr) = An accomplished fact
Dulce et decorum est pro patria mori
(L) = It is sweet and noble to die for one's country

Welch Jeyaraj Balasingam

Egypt Invaded

When the Italians invaded I was in command as my Platoon Commander PSM Percy Smith was in Palestine where his wife was expecting a baby. Our forces had no intention of staying near the border of Libya to engage with the Italians when they entered Egypt but moved further east. When our company was leaving, the Company Commander left me to take up a position on a ridge overlooking the road from Libya to Egypt. The road, shortly after entering Egypt, ran through a fairly large area of salt marsh. I was to carry out rearguard action if necessary. It was when the Italians entered Egypt 9/9/40.

The enemy were led by their motorcycle unit, the Bersaglieri. I waited until they were well along the marsh before I gave the order to open fire, at a range of two thousand yards. With our machine guns we skittled them like ninepins.

After a time the enemy started shelling our ridge, when a dispatch rider came to tell me to rejoin the company. We could hear them shelling for some time after we had left. When we reached the company, the Company Commander, Major Forbes-Watson, came to me and said, 'As one hobo to another, congratulations, Sgt Hogg, you are the first commander to engage the enemy on Egyptian soil,' and shook my hand. The Platoon Commander returned two days later and I resumed Platoon Sergeant's duties.

I returned home in October 1943, after seven years in North Africa without home leave, in time for the D-Day landings. PSM Percy Smith was killed in the Middle East on 15/4/45. I wonder if he ever saw his child again.

Robert Hogg

Birdsong

Today I heard birdsong sweet and clear
Telling me secrets and this voice I could hear
Talking about life and where to nest
The bird stretched his wings, puffing his chest
So I reckon, you should hear him too
His song will make you smile if he sings for you.

Charlotte Ekpaloba

The Great Fire Of London

And the fire flew over town and talk
Far swifter than the Duke of York
And he with all his mighty men
Tried stopping its advance in vain

From Tower Bridge the flames rose high
A glowing arch to span the sky
From roof to roof, from wall to wall
The tongues of fire consumed it all

The lighters on the river Thames
Upon the water shone like gems
With goods the boats from aft to bower
Went gently through a fire drop shower

The ash fell on the waves and wakes
With sulphur drops and burning flakes
And all the houses rising higher
Were swiftly swallowed by the fire

Against this blaze there is no proof
From touching slates, from roof to roof
Its smoke spreads wide a blackened sea
And all my thought is, w*oe is me!*

Down by the banks and busy docks
The distant fire burns and mocks
A tear rolls down my glowing cheek
This fire will take both strong and weak

I've buried all my gold and chattel
From all this hot and bloody battle
And all the souls within my pay
I've seen them all get safe away

And now there's me old Samuel Pepys
For London town my old heart weeps
May God himself the heavens rend
And bring this blaze unto an end

How strange a spark in Pudding Lane
Should cause such heartache, loss and pain
To raze this ancient city down
To burning ash in London town

Seth Murti

Dignity

Dignity is the elevation of aspect,
A state of worthiness,
Or having a high-sounding name,
Like Lord Horatio Nelson of Naval fame.
But we can't all be admirals,
Or dukes of royal birth,
We are born with our feet set firmly,
On this common earth.
Nevertheless Dignity can belong to us,
If we stand still like a Redwood tree,
And treat our fellow citizens,
With honour and humility.
Dignity is not ours from birth,
But how we treat others through our life,
With an absence of anger, trouble or strife,
Treat each human being with an equal smile,
Then dignity will become ours forever.

Horatio

The Table Of Life

Bluebells and snowdrops of spring
A blossom of white and of pink
In the light, to paint from a canvas of white.
The allure of a distant green hillside
Through nature's forest far and wide
The flakes that glisten and remind us of today
The mountain with which the mists hide the peaks
Down through the valley where this poet speaks

That song that plays.
At distance now.
A memory of you that stays.
The roses sit in the garden and wait
Dancing in the breeze of late.
That song still plays, a memory of you.
Where only a memory casts those roses adrift
Those yellow-red tulips, the rain shadow shift.
Sit and watch the sweet flower grow
The flower amidst the sweet scented meadow
Dahlia sit beside the daisy shed
Beside the strawberries and the tulip bed.

A dahlia for the memory
An evening primrose where I sleep
The rainfall of June and July.
A peace rose that sits in the mind,
The crocus, the marigold we leave behind.
The water under the bridge,
The flood waters racing beneath
A yellow rose with its petals
The spiteful frost of autumn's loom
Like love taken away too soon.

I am the bee upon the flower
Hovering with coloured winged butterflies
Gathering pollen by the hour.
After dark clouds are the blue skies.
Each raindrop that glistens, splash and fall
Through the sunlight glows a rainbow
Past the bluebottle, that some hold windows
Like the ivy that creeps up the garden wall.

Like remembrance of seasons of immortality
From spring the gathering of blossoms fly.
Rain like teardrops from the darkness until neigh
Like the humble bumblebee that smiles
Of England in summer bloom.
Time like nurtured vegetables and new life from each seed
The wild flowers, stingers and loathsome weed.

That we can laugh now
That we can laugh now.

Barry Powell

I Don't Care

I watch the news and all I see,
Is hate, lies and misery.
Yet while this proves the world unfair,
It doesn't affect me so I don't care.

I go out into the street,
And see a young man soon to be beat.
And though he could end bound to a chair,
He's not me – so I don't care.

I look in an alley, and with a fright,
See a woman distraught and a man rife with delight.
And although she lay broken and bare,
I turn my head, the act unseen – I don't care.

But this is where the tale twists,
A hooded figure latches onto my wrists.
Asking for money, valuables, yet I am no man of affairs.
A blade to my throat, I scream for help – but no one cares.

Jai Small

Saved By A Whisker

My name is Pussy Pusskin,
I was saved from being drowned,
Someone had put me in a sack,
Then with rope securely bound.

It was dark and I was frightened,
Though I was not alone,
Four of us were in the bag,
Which round was tied a stone.

We were thrown into the river,
We sank so very fast,
Our breath was taken from us,
We knew we couldn't last.

Then almost at our end,
We felt something lift us high,
We were no longer in the water,
We could suddenly see the sky.

A face appeared before us,
We mewed with such relief,
The kind face gently picked us out,
Saved us from our grief.

He put us in his car,
And drove us to his home,
He gently put us on the rug,
Then we heard him on the phone.

We drank the milk he gave us,
It was warm and tasted good,
Then he popped us in a box,
With a blanket as a hood.

We heard a knock upon the door,
A voice said, 'Now, let's see,
These little kittens you kindly saved,
I'll take them back with me.'

We're being cared for in a home,
So lucky to be alive,
There are many other animals who,
With your help will, too, survive.

Monica Buxton

Sound Of The Trinket

Behold the thought of a curious sound
Dripping eloquently all around
Reckoning through amidst the tides
Feeling like a burden as if to thrive
Our ears are open to tendencies
Not hope, forgiveness and clemency
Lost in the world of our dug up cradle
Reach out to grasp divinity's aid
Ears crackle to unheard trinkets
Listen carefully to absorb its message
Carefully patented to adhere to your tears
Majestically eloquent to crave you a new heir
Indulge yourself to its acoustics
Only then may you decrypt its linguistics!

Amir Motlagh

Confessions Of A Cleaner

This is my life
I wake up in the ghetto
I can't be a secretary
I can't be a clerk
So I sit back and wonder
What can I do.

I pick up my mop
I pick up my bucket
And I start to clean
Mopping, cleaning, thinking
What can I do?
Baby needs new clothes
Baby needs new shoes
What can I do?
What can I do?

The pot's on the fire
And the foods not enough
Trust me.

Mopping, cleaning, thinking
What can I do?
I can't go back to school
Education is dear
But no time to spare.

I start to think
What can I do?
What can I do?
And there it was
The bucket in my left hand
The mop in my right
And so I became a cleaner.

H A Finnah

Exploration

Exploration of the body
Exploration of the mind
Which of these two paths
Will show what there is to find?
Man in his seeking
Has in his quest no inkling,

The treasures to be found
The body, is it sound,
Or do we use it and abuse it,
A God given gift to seek, to find
Treasures around our world
Or are we too much in a whirl?

Exploration of the mind
Slow down, take your time,
Visit the deepest recesses
Don't do things to excess,
Sit quietly, ponder your next move
Is it one of which God would approve?

Reach out to the community
Enjoy interaction happily,
Our road is set before us
To enjoy God's love, so glorious.

Elizabeth Adams

Celebrations

Friends and comrades and fellow countrymen
Listen; oh listen to the voice of joy,
How gallant men, cooks and men of the pen
Have destroyed the foe, and given much to enjoy.

Such was the zeal in their warm fervent heart,
Such was the passion that ran through their veins.
These and much much more set them all apart
They fought and sprained to give us no more pain.

We are happy, always now and today,
For we have laughter, freedom, health and store,
Rabbits are happy in their ***clapier***,
And to each we turn with much more ***amour***.

Let the bright, happy balloons fly, pour drinks,
Together we dance, eat and share a wink.

Kumbi Johnson

Butterfly Of Reflection

Butterfly of reflection upon a flower you love to rest,
You love to dance at nature's request,
Fluttering your wings so fragile,
The gentle breeze whispers to you,
You make everyone smile,
You love the sunkissed blue sky
And everything that reflects as you flutter on by,
The birds sing to you in each bright new day,
You love to daydream along the way,
To colourful flowers that grow in the sunkissed earth,
In spring's rebirth.

Joanna John

A Child's Game (When We Were Young)

Oh! When we were children
Such games we would play.

We would live out our fantasy
Day after day.

Pirates or cowboys
Those stories we told.

And
How we all thought, we would never grow old.

Where have they all gone now
Those friends we once knew?

Cast off our memories
Like old clothes we outgrew

Play conkers in autumn
Pick daisies in June.

Holding hands in the playground.
Lick jam from the spoon.

High tea on a Sunday.
Cream teas
Oh! What a sight.

Maths test tomorrow.
Egg and chips Wednesday night.

Looking out the window
Get a clip around the ear.

But school's out forever
At the end of the year.

David Carter

Imagine!

Do others feel great sadness,
When the sky is overcast?
Is that the time imagination
Leads to lands quite vast?

Do pictures flash across your thoughts,
Of islands far away?
Do you pretend to climb the waves,
On a surfboard, in the bay?

Maybe you watch cool waterfalls,
Leaping from great heights,
Then walk, in spring, amidst the flowers
And trees, with great delight.

Maybe you visualise the fêtes,
Assembled at your school,
Or the birthday parties of your friends,
With cakes to make one drool.

And once there were the pantomimes,
Where you could act a part,
Or chairs with voices singing,
That stole your parents' hearts.

So when the snow is falling,
Though the sky and sun are bright,
Think back to all the wondrous things,
That, in the past, delight!

Nola Small

Silver Sky Castle

Love me now, together live
With the joys the world can give
Streets, parks and market squares
The friends and family we have there
  Upon a wall sit hand in hand
  See the peasants work the land
  Stacks of hay where swallows play
  A sunny song that greets the day
    Brew a perfume sweetly thin
    To add a garden to your skin
    A fragrance rich of summer morn
    Enough to make me glad I'm born

Clothes of silk from shops we buy
To look our best in hot July
With money earned from jobs we do
Spend my precious wage on you
  Feathered pillows, luxurious sheets
  Sea chest treasures and golden fleets
  Blessed in faith daylight ends
  Beside me now my love ascends
    We shall build a nest up there
    A castle of silver in mid air
    If this is all she asks of me
    Then be my love and live with me

Rodger Moir

The Battle Of Britain

Again we remember those September days in the 1940s.
Again we remember, with honour and pride . . .

Inspired by thought of liberty . . .
Salvation, hope and peace,
Throughout the day our 'pilots' fought,
A freedom to release.

Conquesting elements of war . . .
In spacious realms of blue,
Above the fields of burnished corn . . .
From dawn to dusk they flew.

Their courage overcame their fears . . .
Brave, gallant, bold and true,
Again we honour them with pride,
So mighty were 'those few'.

Malcolm Wilson Bucknall

My Four Seasons

Behold! This summer glade,
Where budded spring, her foliaged change hath made,
And left each living leaf and flower to tell
Of wondrous things, by nature wrought,
Above the arts of man; within his thoughts to dwell.

Next cometh autumn, whose leaves, her mantle lay
Upon the soft sweet bosom of the Earth,
To soak in nature's hues,
To mingle with November's dews
And scent each shortening day.

Now winter! dark, dank, dreary so it seems;
White snow with frills of frost, through which a sun-shaft beams
To brighten and to lift the downcast mind,
To warm away the chill of winter's wind
And 'mind us of the thrill of spring's own dreams.

At last! comes spring, with promise of a newborn year:
Of life anew, replenished and refreshed and free from fear;
And all our youth comes forth in grand review
To pass again before us, and renew
Acquaintance with the child that once we were.

Geoffrey Cope

Red Kites

Red kites shining in the sky
We're looking up, watching them fly
Out of their surreal world
Loudspeaker for a hidden word.
Drifting across the horizon
Shadowy shapes we fix our eyes on
What a sight to behold
On this dream we are sold.

In and out of the clouds
High above the watching crowds.
A misty dream, we can barely see
But we know it relates to destiny.
A tug on the rope, going higher yet
A captured dream, we will never forget.
Floating into our heads
Seeing different shades of red.

As we take a different view
Such a sight could never be blue.
Hypnotic overtures enter our minds
Arranged in symmetrical lines.
Red kites sailing in the sky
We're looking up, watching them fly
Out of their special world.
Will we ever discover, the hidden words?

Ian Bosker

Trees In Bedwellty Park No 6

Those aged young men are not present here,
This memorial post, where tear marked weeping trees slumber.

In a passing heart, the names of those inattentive parade.
At the ready to depart, disperse like the rattle of yellow smoke, and echoed by whistles.

Tredegar's war dead simply can't.

Take me to the conclusion of artillery guns, that smack the fear into those with breathless lungs, as absent as meat and bones.

Take me to the men let slip and through and up and over parapet.

Take me to the slaughter of infantry advancing in good and hopeful order, where sweetened bullets sting and sing and scythe, and bayonets bend in homage of a parted cage.

Take me where the horses scream while pulling rifled steel, the strength of iron failed, and surrounding forces squeeze with pressurised discord.

Take me to the death of time as witnessed by relentless restless ticking assembly production line.

Take me to those feathers stuck that killed the unquiet, quietly quick, of those whose ribbons bite through blood and frightened muck.

Yet here, empty wound healed cleared sky and now, where warmth is love, and love a clause of life's time, at this sleep, the last green rest, in remembrance of those in low deep, and still, and still.

David Pierce

The Secret Life Of Toys

Our toys get into mischief when we are all asleep
Teddy bangs his big bass drum, gets them on their feet
Jess, the little pony, prances in the door
Dolls put on their dancing shoes caper round the floor
Fleur, the ballerina, makes graceful twists and twirls
Mick, a naughty monkey, teases all the girls
Annabelle, the baby, bouncing in her cot
Gus, the grumpy camel (he's always in a strop)
Miss Molly's in her kitchen stirring up a brew
Spotty Dog and Bunnikins playing tag with Roo
Tim, the crafty kitten, has found a hiding place.
Soldiers in smart uniforms all marching back to base
Sam the jolly sailor brings 'Queenie' into port
Storms and even hurricanes, forecasters soon report
Wise Old Owl is listening, he gives a warning call
Back into your places, it's morning one and all.
So if your toys seem sleepy in the morning light
Just remember children, that they party every night.

Doreen Goodway

Our Sun-Blind

When it's summer and is hot
We put our sun-blind on the door
It's red and white and striped
My grandma had it long before
But when the sun has gone and is no more
Back it goes into store
Some say how very English
What is a sun-blind for?
Well to stop the paint from blistering
That's why we put it on our door

Pauline Kavanagh

Ode To Richard

Historians say that he fought the good fight –
Our King with crooked spine, and build so slight,
Slain on Bosworth Field – as everyone knows –
Felled from his horse, with humiliating blows.
This much-maligned man, this legendary King,
(Our Uni gave the world his DNA fingerprinting)
Was portrayed as a tyrant, but he didn't fail
To give us more books, and the system of bail.
With skull and skill they've reconstructed his face,
Whilst controversy reigns – his final resting place.
However most think it's a wonderful thing
After 500 years – we know it's our King – found
'Neath a Leicester car park, in a deep hole,
The last Plantagenet – God rest his soul!

Janet Peberdy

Us (Together)

I saw his face, his shining smile
That look of happiness was just his style.
The quiet wink as he looked at me
Was given in secret for only me to see

His love was true, yes, very real
It was true love without a deal
It was from his heart and just for me
And I returned my love as true love should be

But although he has now gone my true love will stay
No man can replace him in anyway
For 57 years our true love was strong
Now although he is in Heaven
My true love will go on.

Bonnie Austin

The Woodland One

By summer greens and autumn browns
And snow-white winter hoods,
Come spring bluebells perfumed around
Go I, the one of the woods.

By emerald walks and falling leaves
And starlight frosted skies,
Hawthorn dawns and scented breeze
Through woodlands wander I.

By buzzing of bees on daffs of yellow
And the stretching of trees in bud.
Calls of the cuckoo and first of swallow
Go I, the one of the woods.

By shades of jade and cornflake tread
And ponds with skaters on.
Larks that sing from overhead,
Go I, the woodland one.

By sunshine's gold and mists of grey
And silvery streams that flood,
Where nature dreams come spring imps play
Go I, the one of the woods.

Peter Ridgway

The North Sea

I went to see the sea, cold, dark and grey it glowered back at me,
'I have your treasures buried underneath, your buildings,
everything you need, to be.'

'I'm waiting for you out here,' said the sea,
'I eat your cities through eternity,
do not draw near, my waves are quite bereft of sympathy.'

'My cold breath takes your warmth and turns it blue,
I have no pity for the likes of you in any hue.'

'Dare ride upon my cold white surf awhile,
for I can wait until you cannot smile.'

'Crosses from old abbeys lost in time,
Lay low in comfort washed by my cold brine.'

'Swords from Vikings, Angles, Saxon, crested hilts with
stones you cannot find upon my beach,
for centuries they will be out of reach.'

'But when my waves draw blankets over you in my own devil's brew,
Some other folk will see who never knew.'

'We stand and face each other for a while,
but, waves erode your footprints and I'm driven
back to dry in nature's style.'

Jean Paisley

The Voice

'Hilary is pregnant!' What?… I turned round sharply, but, quite incredibly, no one was there. How could that be? 'The voice' was distinctly male, soft and angelic spoken. However, there was nothing else said, which led me to think it was maybe my imagination.

Totally bewildered, I shivered inwardly. Clutching Hilary's hand, we continued walking on the eerie, unlit path, which wound through the cathedral's ancient gravestones and yew trees.

We had just been at the Christmas Eve Nightwatch Service and Hilary, my wife, was apparently unaware of my peculiar, audible message. Remembering as well that tests had proved it practically impossible for her to have children, I never mentioned the incident and totally forgot about it.

The festivities passed and one day at the end of January, I arrived home to find Hilary looking radiant. 'John – great news!' she said, 'I'm ***six*** weeks pregnant!'

I was gobsmacked to say the least. Not only by the medical fact, but also, I remembered what 'the voice' had said ***five*** weeks ago… So it wasn't my imagination?

A few years later, I was made redundant and life became increasingly difficult in many ways.

Then last Sunday evening, accompanied by Hilary and our young son Jonathan, I was walking along that same creepy path from the cathedral, when I was yet again suddenly chilled with elated disbelief, by that same, angelic voice, which softly stated, 'Don't despair… millionaire!'

Hunter Buchanan

A Place Like Eden

When the sun first charmed the ocean
And the warmth formed the clouds above
Earth, sea, wind and fire
Kindled with eternal love
God is a spirit, He is all around
Our Saviour Jesus first taught all
Be it giants of the Old Testament
Or the lowly sparrows small
Love is, was and always will be
The essence of a blissful life
When God gave us milk and honey
And the water turned to wine
Everything in life gets better
When we ask and we receive
When we knock and the door will open
When we first come to believe
When the sun first charmed the ocean
And from nought all came to be
Eden is a special place
A garden of love made especially
For you, for me and all creation
When we come to take the test
Whoever loves will ne're be forsaken
And will find eternal rest.

Christine Parker

Family Of Only Brothers

My family was my lifeline all those years ago,
We mingled in together like a big old bedroom throw,
It didn't seem to matter what time of day it was,
We would just be a family, that's how it would go,
Life was so easy and carefree all the time,
It didn't seem so long ago we were all there in mind,
Love surrounded us whichever way we turned,
It was happiness in abundance, that is just a word,
Words came flowingly and without a care,
We would go through life not thinking,
If we would always be there.
Of course reality became the norm,
And life took on a different form,
There became more of us and the family grew and grew,
There wasn't time to stand and stare it was always there.
Some of our family passed away,
That is life on Earth today, it is a sorrow and a pain.
But we learn to mourn and go on our way,
Make love a thing that lasts and lasts,
Because that is all we can ask.

Iris Crew

Untitled

Barcelona is a city
Waiting for Costas.
The yellow canary
Looks out for him in the darkness.
There is nobody to embrace at dawn
Words remain unsaid,
Such silence!

Sandra Lynne Grayson

The Sadness Of War

A hundred years ago this year, our young men went to war,
Because they thought Great Britain was worth fighting for.
Each Tom, Dick, Harry and Jack, didn't think that they wouldn't be coming back.
They went into battle in trenches full of mud, into hails of bullets,
shrapnel and comrades' blood.
Passchendaele, Ypres and the Somme, millions of men died in those foreign fields,
Thousands of gravestones, sad reminders of the horrors that battle yields,
In the fields of Flanders, where poppies grew, now a yearly reminder
that makes us remember,
The sacrifice all those soldiers made, every 11th of November,
Yet still our men go out to fight in foreign lands,
to bring stability and peace, if they can.
Some of them are dying in Afghanistan, trying to free the country from the Taliban.
Soon they will be leaving that country to its own devices,
hoping strife will cease,
And all the Afghan people will forever live in peace,
but I'm afraid, I'm afraid they won't get release.
There will always be bombings and killings, wrought by terrorists who come if they can.
We have tried, we have shown the way, we have done all that we can.
What for? This is the sadness of war.

Kenneth V Jackson

Untitled

'Purl Knitters' we are called
And we knit for charity,
Knitting, chat and coffee!
And 'blessed' living by the sea!

Sandy

It's So Hard To Believe

(Dedicated to:- All those who died . . . the poor victims
those who tried . . . the rescue teams
those who cried . . . good people everywhere)

I read in a book of fishes and loaves
Of water being turned into wine
How God sent his Son, the saviour of men
To teach us the word and the sign.

Parables, miracles, and wonderful deeds
Seas parting to let people through
All things that we could we did cos we should
Do to others as they would do to you.

But how can I believe there's a God up above
Who cares for us all as they say
When suicide terrorists kill too many to list
On September 11th Tuesday.

Four planes left the ground, oblivion bound
The passengers all unaware
Of carnage untold about to unfold
Planned by lunatics hidden somewhere.

Ten minutes into flight, sounds of a fight
The pilots and crews overcame
The planes altered course, no sign of remorse
Flown by killers who all thought the same

In uptown New York, folk left home for work
Not knowing just what lay ahead
Planes rammed the Trade Towers, starting huge fires
Now thousands of people are dead.

Two thousand eight hundred and thirty seven
Innocent victims died
In a huge Holocaust, every single life lost
As helpless rescuers just stood and cried

Religious fanatics did this dreadful deed
This world is a terrible place
Osama Bin Laden the Devil Incarnate
Enemy of the whole human race.

If good is to prevail, Lord please do not fail
Stamp out this evil within
As you did long ago, please give us a sign
Cos my faith really is wearing thin.

Yes, it's so hard to believe, as I see people grieve
For atrocities done, man to man
But I guess that I must, in God place my trust
For if anyone can, only He can.
Save the human race.

Robert W M Bassett

The Shooting Star

All day the rising temper of the wind
Attacks the elms cross-hatched against the sky,
Dusk falls early, the earth grows cold where the green apples lie,
And cawing rooks rise upward from their roost
In noisy discourse when the day has fled,
The house falls silent and, withdrawn, dreams dance inside my head.
From its secure cocoon my spirit slips,
Enters another quadrant and finds there
Freed from the bonds of place and time, all joy, compassion, care.
Drawn to a radiance clearer than the sun,
A form of strength besides which such a frail
Image of my unstructured life appears snow-berry pale.
A momentary gathering to Himself,
A cleansing, healing, heavenly touch of fire
Returns me earthward this October night, a shooting star.

Artscape

Ecstasy

Deep breath fling wide my arms embracing space,
Elation surges sparkles from my eyes.
Back dropped by peaks with cloud wisps on each face
Brown heathered moors stretch miles beneath flared skies.
Remoteness pleases me, I'm galvanised
Among these rounded hills unchanged down years,
By roistering winds I'm charged and energised.
A champagne cork of joy bursts in me here
I want to stay and wish the earth would stall.
When I put up a startled grouse or hare
Find primroses beside the waterfall
My day is made, I linger just to stare,
Then snail like follow where the sheep tracks wind
Down to the world I'd gladly leave behind.

Pam Russell

Canute Country

More flowers must stun dreams
for wishers in yesterdayland
if they are to venerate an improbable land
where wishes don't come true.
It cools off after six and threatens
to make life difficult whichever
way you look at it like some
prison warden of Zenda desperate
for the internment of Zephyrus.
Or anyone attempting to buy genius
must sojourn in hell for a bet
they cannot win until ten years dead
if that sounds forced to you
keep looking over your shoulder.

John Dillon

On The Beach

I'm going to the seaside
To catch the warming sun.
There's lots of other people
Here to have some fun.

A father and his daughter
Bury Mum up to her neck.
Then they walk into the waves
To search a sunken wreck.

Boy and Dad upon the rocks
With bucket look for crabs.
When they're tired and hungry
They go home in a cab.

Thirsty beauty on the beach
In T-shirt and no bra.
Two points on her licence
If she finds a bar.

A blonde is sleeping on the sand
She has a blue bikini.
A crowd begins to gather round
Because it is so teeny.

Brightly coloured ice cream vans
Are scattered far and wide.
Parking on the muddy sand
They watch the rising tide.

Walking on the cliff tops
Where seagulls turn and dive.
I offer them my sandwich bread
And dozens have arrived.

Out West the sun is setting
There's sunburn on my hips.
Time to end a lovely day
With salty fish and chips.

R E Thorne

B-Cup Blues

Please let me be, oh how I wanna be a 'B' cup.
But they just keep growing and flowing
and now they're a double 'D' cup.

They started creeping gradually,
I pretended not to see.
I'd diet, they'd subside gracefully
but then grew to a double 'D'!

They're climbing out of tasteful lace
where they're supposed to be encased
– they climbed right out of 'B's and 'C's
where they used to sit with ease.

Belching out like giant pies
oven baked with too much rise.
They're growing right before my eyes
and I just want . . . a 'B' cup.

– Swollen vests and lumpy jumpers
greet me as I dress each day.
Girls pay for breasts like mine
but I want them to shrink right down,
so now I pray . . . and pray to be
a sweet, neat cup size 'B'!

Gabrielle Alexander

Ice Cream

We each had an ice cream.
For a moment time turned a blind
eye to our pleasure.
The sea roughed and roared,
pummelled and slapped its briny
hands against the shore,
but no power on Earth could
spoil our fun.
The hot sun did its best to melt
your vanilla whip and my honeycomb
crunch, but each sticky runnel
and creamy drip improved the taste.
All the words we spoke were
coated in unctuous flavour.
I took a lick of your vanilla
whip and you a bite of my
honeycomb crunch,
and we laughed at a dog chasing
its tail on the beach.

Paul Jones

Tree, Tree, Tree

O tree, tree, tree, how wise I would be
if I could live as long as thee. Old tree
where birds find their rest in thee old
tree and men make beautiful things
from thee, old tree, for cities could not
be built without thee, old tree. I
wonder where men would be without
thee, old tree. Thy beauty is to see,
for man's 5 senses can be found in
thee, old tree, of taste, see, smell,
hear, feel, the breeze blowing through
thee and hear the winds whistling
through thee and taste thy fruits, old
tree and to smell thy blossom that
flowers in May and to feel thy rough
bark and smooth thing that men can
make with thee, old tree. Yes, man's
life here on Earth would be so much
poorer without thee, my old friend, the tree.
Yes, how wise I would be if I could live
as long as thee, old tree, tree, tree.

John Brian

The Weather Forecast

How should I dress?
Glassy winter clothes
or summer dripping wet ones?
Umbrellas, boots or galoshes?
Perhaps a parasol?

How should I dress?
Ghosts on satellite images
on the TV weather forecast
a starched sky for now
plastic stickers on the map.

How should I dress?
The presenter holds on
wailing hot and pounding feet
on the melting tarmac
filtered cold, clasped and twisted.

How should I dress?
Skater in the night or in a daydream
innocent destinations on a map
the weather?
Just another thought!

Mariana Zavati

A Christmas Tale In Rhyme

I plodded on, my annual duel,
To combat Christmas shopping,
The queues were just like pulling teeth,
With crying children moping.
'Christmas present number one',
Would I be defeated?
The list was more than twenty yards,
'Stuff them,' Scrooge then bleated.
Bobbing heads surrounded me,
A sea of frenzied shoppers,
In colourful clothes they lugged their bags,
Nothing else much mattered.
After present three or four,
A 'Santa' came in sight,
He may be fooling little kids,
But not me, in my plight,
I'd gladly sit upon his knee,
If he'd then do my shopping,
He'd have my list, he'd have his legs,
To bloody send him trotting.
Now I'm feeling well hacked off,
My arms are stretched and ache,
I might stop off at Burger King,
Or collapse for goodness sake,
With a cuppa down my chute,
I'm ready for leg two,
The list is 'boggled eyed' to me,
And now I need the loo.
Cramming in all bloody day,
Aching for a nap,
When now I've got on top of it,
I have to take that crap.
Suddenly an OAP,
Came belting in my way,
I swear that she was quite possessed,
And causing an affray,
Her wheely-buggy went full blast,
And hit me then full on,
My elbow-hurt, my leg was grazed,

By the time that she was done,
(I said ouch.)
Anyway, at closing time,
Nothing I had missed,
I hope that I'm appreciated,
My family are ungrateful gits.

Next . . .
Back at home I try to squash,
The gifts beneath my bed,
The bloody things, they will go in,
If I end up dead,
Wrapping a mind-blowing job
The tape just sticks to me,
But thumb holes in my wrapping paper,
Hopefully are discreet,
Tags are slightly easier,
Although the pen doth run,
Rather blotchy, rather smudgy,
But this is just a con,
Because most have a sticker saying
'Santa Claus' did send it,
I've just been dashing all over,
When that moron gets full credit,
However, some gifts are for family,
Although the foresaid gits,
Auntie Mrytle is the worst,
For us she bloody knits.
One for all, and all for one,
What to choose or not,
Every time I get it wrong,
My head is on the block.
Tomorrow will be broken toys,
Rejects, and much fretting,
The tension just like World War Three,
And more, that's what I'm betting.

Denise Oldale

Where You Are

When I think of home
It's always going to be
There where you are
And if I follow my heart
It will always bring me back
To where you are

When I've been out there
In the wind and the rain
Then your love is the reason
I'll be coming back home
To your heart once again

When I think of home
It's always going to be there
Where you are
And if I follow my heart
It will always bring me
Back to where you are.

K Lake

Sunrise

The sun is rising o'er the sea;
A magic moment just for me,
A holy peace rests in the air;
A dazzling light floods everywhere.
The tide laps gently against the wall;
Seabirds cry out with ecstatic call.
This is the triumph of the light,
That drives away the gloom of night.
This is a very blessed morn,
Just like the day when Christ was born.
The sun is rising o'er the sea;
And in my heart, God speaks to me.

P Mitchell

Double-Deckered London Bus

Through my window
I can see inside the bus.
From the safety of my lazy lacy room
I get a dekko in the double-decker.

A London morning brings out every type,
Early risers on their way to work:
Multi-skilled, multi-racial, multi-coloured,
Boiler-suited, uniformed, sensibly clad against the elements.

Though I can't see or hear, I'm sure
'More room on top' echoes from below,
And, as it lurches in its double-deckered drive,
I can imagine those who stand 'inside'!

On top the gazers lift their eyes once more
As, laden with its load, it groans again,
And from my window I can see the faces
Anxious in their double-deckered anticipation.

Anna Liffey

Twilight Of Perchance

Sea's grace possessing hue in day's adieu,
Swells sky's entrance, vaults in the stars astound,
As sun's dipped glow now reels the night in due,
To shade light's play rose lipped in touch dark's found,
Where ocean's sweep implores perpetual weep,
In cadence soft on reap's cloyed pebble's shore,
Whose gentle waves ascend and push to peep,
Then in recess do rush to dash a more.
And in this scene hush tranquil in eyes thou,
How firefly lamps incense across the bay,
Shine in minds aura of this depthless now,
This darkness still this blest such peace convey.
And I who daze in twilight of perchance,
Dream in wonder's trance lost in gaze's glance.

Barry Bradshaigh

Returning Friends

I saw my friends again today.
Returned, from winter in the sun.
Darting here and there and everywhere,
to see what projects had begun,
since last they graced these shores.

They left last year in autumn time.
Melting into morning's mist.
Without a word or hint to me,
whose life they had so warmly kissed,
in summer's endless days.

And I was left in winter's drear
to wait for spring in solitude.
Yet, with that poet's inward eye,
could gaze on pleasure long removed,
and see again my dears.

The year has turned full circle round.
Spring bursts forth in sheer delight,
with promises of birth and life.
And oh! what joy in morning's light,
the swallows have returned.

Jeanette Allen

Did You Ever Go Conkering Dad?

Just over the road from where Nan lives
Through a couple of rough talking alleys
Out onto the fields and swings
Into the forests beyond
That's where we'd go conkering

There were lots more then
Up to our knees in them we were
No need to throw a stick up
They all fell off in the same week
Every year, without fail

Bring them home to show Nan
She'd bake a few and pickle a few
Give us a head start in the playground
Until Jonesy got his dad to drill a hole
In a small pebble he'd painted brown.

Steven Savage

The Fourth Sign Of The Zodiac

Sarcoma
rolling through life's blood
through me
oh just shoot me
I may cry all the same
destruction and death
be my bane

I will not see the bluebells in April,
the rabbits in the hedgerow
nor the campion and primrose
as this seething snake,
journeys
through the labyrinth of my vessels and veins
dormant
it then leaps at the barricades

my body;
a constellation of cancer
it dominates my every thought
cancroid, pernicious
it invades my body
and punctures my heart

a solid tumescent mass
without a definitive shape
complex and thoughtless
it arrives with silent grace

what happened?
Someone knocked at the door
I answered
in came sarx
hidden; behind a mask

it does not beseech me
it decides; of its own volition
to claim me
to take me away.

Sadly we are not made of such particles that forever last
yet we enrich the earth
long after we decay.

S.A.A.

Apart

Whenever we are apart
You will always be in my heart
Together like a horse and cart
If I were to lose you I would surely smart
I loved you right from the start

When people see us they stare
They know, for each other, we care
You are a dream and no nightmare
For you I have plenty of time to spare
Together we make the perfect pair

You were sent from the heavens above
You come to me like a beautiful white dove
Showering me with your tender, affectionate love

I love you girl, I truly do
And I would do anything for you
Whatever you want me to

I love you girl, ever so much
And as each day passes
I can feel your warm, tender, loving touch

I love you each and every day
And I hope you will never go away
With me you will always stay

I have plenty of love for you, on that you can bet
And I will never make you unhappy or upset
So you have no need to worry and never need to fret.

Wally

Heaven Sent

I raised my eyes towards the sky
Gasping painfully for a last sigh
Hoping for a sign from Heaven
A special blessing God sent

My eyes blurred in desperation
As night cast a shadow of desolation
Over the only wish never answered
The precious dream turned into a prayer

As I laid my tired eyes to rest
Praying for a miracle as I know best
A blissful of colours flashed before me
A constellation of stars was facing me

Each bearing a message so divine
That my life was about to shine
Heaven was opening his arms to embrace me
The stars have aligned to rescue me
With glory and majesty like a gift heaven sent.

Star

Weeping Willow Trees By The Hoggsmill River

The wonder of the weeping willow so big and
tall with branches like long arms hanging low –
I look and see you are ready to meet an endless
flowing stream – your cover of leaves come and
disappear as the seasons change – leaving the waters
to flow endlessly on its never-ending quiet quest to
reach the open sea.

Rowland Scannell

A Farmer To His Son

Look over there, in that field of corn,
By the shady tree, my shire was born
And we ploughed the fields from dusk till dawn, boy,
Yes from dusk till dawn.

The years went by so quickly, and all around did change,
This field where life was made, was somehow rearranged,
And now it's a grange, boy,
Yes now it's a grange!

There's so much beauty in this land, of that we can see each day,
But money, it speaks in volumes, and this beauty is taken away,
No more fields to make the hay, boy,
No more fields to make the hay.

When you see the land being built on, and fields going one by one,
Go back to the olden days, when these fields were bathed in sun,
The smell of the hay, a beautiful day!
And a good day's work was done, boy,
And a good day's work was done.

So remember as you go through life, be kind and help where you can,
These fields of gold, precious memories they hold,
Can be taken with a snatch of the hand, boy,
Can be taken with the snatch of the hand.

Remember my shire, born under the tree?
Many years of service she gave to me
And when it was her time to leave . . .
It broke my heart and I did grieve, boy,
Yes . . . it broke my heart and I did grieve.

Memories born, and memories lost,
In our lives what does it cost?
This land we love, is it here to stay,
Like a summer breeze, will it blow away?
Will farmer and son, live life for today,
Or turn their backs and walk away,
Or turn their backs and walk away.

Yvette Clegg

Searching For A Winning Poem

I can't claim to be a William Shakespeare or Blake
I have no idea where my imagination will take
Me – I could try my hand at alliteration
This could make my poem a sensation.
Try digging deep into the recesses of my brain
Great ideas and thoughts I may have, but remain
Undiscovered at present: perhaps later my pen will come to the fore
But I must not, I will not ignore
The challenge to be the best poet in twenty-fourteen –
The prize may go to one who is barely sixteen.

Ideas come and also go
Like plants I have to nurture them until they grow
But time and again I need to reform
Them so that it's perfect in word and shape
Making sure that others will stand and gape
At my poetical skill
And my poem reaches the top of the bill
To be counted amongst the renowned
Proclaiming: 'A new talent has been found!'

Patricia J Tausz

Glamour Puss Or Glamour Pigeon

... or sex kitten for that matter! They seem to pop up everywhere and not a day goes by without coming across one... according to my other half that is.
On one of his latest assignments, he had to deal with a lady who was wearing the shortest skirt possible. Nothing wrong with wearing a short skirt you'll say and I agree. But when said lady is bent over, re-arranging cushions on the sofa and thereby baring all... well almost all, as she was wearing a bum-floss-type-undergarment... where do you look? He said he just carried on with his work, doing his very best to avert his eyes... I believe him... ahem!
Come to think of it, I wonder if I should start to get worried about all these encounters. Only the other day, himself comes home and tells me about his day.
'And there was this young-ish, recently divorced lady telling me her friends are trying to convince her to go to Thailand and she made a promise to herself to say yes to everything...'
Himself also mentioned that the lady in question was wearing nothing but the flimsiest of dressing gowns. Maybe she just got out of the shower or something... or something indeed!
I'm sure everyone bumps into these, let's call them fashionistas, from time to time. Even my colleagues have experienced them. The woman 'dressed' in barely-there-vest and thong... or the man who opened the door to my (female) colleague, wearing his best budgie smugglers...

Martine Finn

The Gifts Of Mother Nature

Bathed in the early morning dew
Flowers slowly begin to stir
While songbirds herald the day anew
In the crisp morning air

While rippling mountain streams
Meander to the sea
Like endless dreams
Longing to be free

Such beauty to behold
On a summer's day
As drifting clouds unfold
And slowly fade away.

John Mangan

The Cobbles

As I enjoy the quiet rural scene –
a white thatched cottage clad in fragrant flowers
and bask in sunshine which highlights roses
and draw contentment from soft summer showers
which soothe the mind and heighten senses
and see the winding path for passers-by
with hedgerows wreathed in springtime leaves
or summer or autumn or winter's scenery:

for some the way is long and full of pain
as cobblestones are quaint but hard to bear
even when modern feet are stoutly shod.
How much worse then in times gone by
when paupers' feet were often bare
and suffering borne with fortitude?

Gerry Miller

Rhapsody In Blue

I wish that I once more,
Could walk among noble beeches,
Where translucent, infant leaves,
Glow wherever sunlight reaches,

To see bluebells bow in homage,
Beneath the trees so tall and grand,
A woodland scene in Britain,
Becomes a wonder land.

To hear the music of the birds,
Making their springtime claims,
And new arrivals from a distant shore,
Raising a family once again,

If I could wander on the Downs,
Where the chalk escarpment meets the weald,
To see an array of wild flowers,
Whose myriad of colours grace a field.

Above me in a cloudless sky,
The rapid wing beats of a lark,
And circling and soaring way on high,
A hunting buzzard makes her mark.

Where harebells nod on impossible stems,
And a butterfly coming into view,
Fluttering on stunning wings,
Shares with the harebell a similar hue.

Here I am with my memories,
A nature-loving pass-me-by
Whose willing heart, but failing feet,
Is marking time as years pass by,

Now I play at let's pretend,
I have loved the harebells as a friend,
Their gentle beauty I've not forgot,
For now I *grow them in a pot.*

June Worsell

Thump

Become a pedestrian all will be revealed
Hustle, bustle, bump and grind,
Deaf, dopey and slobbish
Ignorant people who pretend to be blind
Have a care now, mind out for that piece of rubbish

Bam, bam, thump

'Keep Britain Tidy'
Was a slogan I once remember –
But fastfood outlets and quickie fix alcohol shops
Do their duty to sell their goods in throwaway cartons, tins and plastic
Which coat the paths and roads with a type of mastic of flotsam and goo
Oh and don't forget the animal poo –
Sometimes so enormous, deposited just outside one's residence –
That one squishes it with one's shoe!

Bam, bam, thump

A stroll to your local shop
One of those that declare pay more, purchase less,
You become waylaid by a 'soda pop'
Who touts 'do ya want business?'
'No. Now, bug off!'

Bam, bam, thump, bam, bam

Now another scrapyard opens
To much chagrin –
'Tis out the way – 'they' say
A magnet for metal delivery dollies
Taken in by speculative chancers.

Bam, bam, thump

Then there is the Ersatz beggar girl
And I've gotten wise to her tricks
Cos I know she only wants money
To obtain drugs for her next fix!
So, nah, nah, nah and no!

Bam, bam, thump

Kids out in the dark, on the street
Till way back when, some as young as six, mayhap, ten –
Parent or parents, having little control over them
Vehicles vandalised, walls graffiti-ised, sirens wailing,
Kids scarpering whilst giving police the finger sign

Bam, bam, thump, bam, bam

Not forgetting the noise
That awakens one during the night with a bump as you clamber from your bed
Bam, bam, thump, bam, bam, thump
You espy the culprits from your windowpane
One of those Boombastic beamers', dark windows, painted red –
A deal done, music (hah) blaring once again –
Bam, bam, thump, bam, bam, thump

An area clean-up
(see cutbacks)

Bam, bam, thump

I'm not a great linguist
As one can plainly see
But having been woken from my dreamladen trist
I'm off to make some tea

Bam, bam, thump
Bam, bam, thump
Goodnight!

Bryan Montague

Poetic Celebrations

Rewards, so many kinds in varied ways,
Annoint the many flavours of our books,
Where poetry, with all its verse and plays,
Enforce the curiosity of looks,
Though compasses in libraries confuse,
Those alphabets of poets passing by,
No longer read, since habits for 'hard news',
Now turns off much attention for globe's eye,
So Browning unto Coleridge depart,
While mighty names repose among the dead,
Like Byron, Blake and Tennyson none start,
From shelves of many libraries, unread!
But why, when England's poetry,
Surpasses every language judged as free?
Sheer sounds are not enough for modern needs,
While countless millions cast themselves away,
To tube-watching, as if discarded seeds,
Imagination lost in parking bay,
Commanding to be found for self's own car,
Removes all inclinations for far more,
'What time's the match? Are we too far?'
To civilise words' process from mailed 'e',
These questions should be asked in many schools,
Before the students pass by quality,
Re-shaped and formed by politicians' rules,
So all those words passed over, shut books' cure,
Pile garbage up for waste lands of manure.
Leave honey from words bees when it arrives,
How fortunate is poet who survives.
Imagine then, what force should we employ,
To spur the British onwards with great cry:
'What's poetry but words which much annoy:
Compelled at school to learn the stuff and sigh,
How long do any scholars have to read,
Assortments from the past and long-dead souls?'
All Britain sets its e-mails up as creed,
For life and work's instruction for all goals?'
These see no 'glare on Skiddaw' in truth's sight,
Macaulay is a saint who has gone by,

Whose works are just remaindered with fools' blight,
Romantically, let Byron enjoy sigh,
Most noble Alexander's locks might grope,
For any sort of rhyming washing soap;
Sometimes does London raise up well-known bridge,
While words of Wordsworth need another sort,
Like Bryon, Keats and Shelley whose verse ridge,
Fast falls below drinks tasting which they brought,
Through quality and quantity of verse,
A fool who wrote today would never see:
Mark now how many publishers rehearse,
Great fear of voices lost in misery,
I may no longer ask 'Sir John' – who's he? –
The Laureate John Betjeman I served,
Above three years and more within TV,
As PR man and publicist preserved,
To aid so many strugglers in light's glare,
While Dylan Thomas needed utmost prayer,
To keep far off the drink within 'BC',
Where Canada did 'stand on guard' – and me,
Around Welsh wizard 'Thomas' constantly
A genius through words, not much to see,
Later he left, so eager for New York:
We should have broken bottles, lost all cork!
Why do so many poets celebrate,
Aware when drunk, wet words wash off fools' slate.

Anthony Russell

Wendy V, Anna And Black B

Born 1820, in Old Catton,
A rural suburb of Norwich,
At only 14 years, Anna Sewell
Was unable to walk through injury,
And needed her family horse,
Usually with carriage, to get around,
As people had to back then.

Anna thus grew to love
The horse and to appreciate
Its vital role in community life,
And so, later on, in the 1870s,
Although bedridden, she penned
Her first and only book,
The evocative 'Black Beauty'.

A portrayal of horse welfare,
Good and bad, uniquely as if seen
Through the eyes of the horse himself,
A tale which has entranced generations
Of children ever since, some of them sufficiently
Into adulthood for a few to establish
Their very own animal welfare charities.

One such local enthusiast,
Wendy Valentine, not only founded,
In 1984, a horse sanctuary, Redwings,
At Frettenham, north of Old Catton,
Now grown to be the largest in UK,
And has rescued many thousands
From neglect, abandonment, and outright cruelty,

But the indefatigable Wendy, in 1995,
Then turned her welfare attentions towards
The dire plight of farm animals, and others,
As victims of barbaric factory production
Methods, and after land purchase nearby,
The Hillside Animal Sanctuary began to nurse
Ill-treated farmed livestock back to health.

This time around, the innovative
Wendy incorporated an undercover operation
To secure evidence, on camera, of cruelty
In action, firm enough to expose, publicise,
And even prosecute the perpetrators, measures
Very distant from the trials of Black Beauty, but
Ones with which his creator would have approved.

Andrew Farmer

Floral Snow

The lovely May-trees
Pink and white,
Made as they moved
An enchanting sight.
But touched by the breezes of early June
May-blossom falleth late or soon,
Their petals falling light,
Floated as leaves by the autumn strewn –
And the lark and thrush burst into tune,
And dawn-gold quenches the morning moon
The green earth grows snow-bright.

As their branches laden
Moved to and fro,
Through the perfumed air
Came falling slow
Fragrant fragments of lovely bloom,
Pink and white, to the earth their tomb;
Ever they float and flow,
Piling thick, some white as the plume
Of the snow-white swan, some pink as the womb
Of an opening rose – and the wind as a broom
Sweepeth the floral snow.

Henry Harding Rogers

Who's A Clever Boy?

I am a dog
My name is Joe
Over the park is where I go
My mistress thinks I'm very clever
For I don't mess in the garden ever
If I'm caught short along the road
Why I just stop, and drop my load
Wherever you go you'll find I've been
For everywhere is my latrine.
I love to beg or fetch a stick
Give a baby's face a lick
Bark at strangers, chase a ball
Chew the doormat in the hall
But when nature calls me to perform
I certainly don't do it on our lawn.
Oh no! I run off quickly to the park
There in a sunlit daisy ring
I lay my steaming mark
So when next you walk
To admire the view
Spare a thought on what we doggies do
Then I think you'll have to admit
Man's best friend is
One hell of a sh*t!

Shirley Nicolaou

Songs Of The Sea

Song of the sea, waves wild and free
Seagull's rebellious cries
Dark clouds reflect on angry waves
Rainbow adorns the sky
Who can still the waves that roll?
Or calm the seagull's cries
Peace to a weary soul tranquillity to searching eyes

God's promised rainbow reflection aglow
From East to West true colours glow
Brightening a wintry sky
Hint of new moon pale and faint, sheltering beside a cloud
Waves steadily roll to an orchestral refrain
Rocks like conductors stand watching the sea wild and free
Haven for waves rolling by.

A boisterous wave thunders o'er the strand
Grand orchestra momentarily stilled
Final vigorous movement as darkness creeps in
Evening's final scene, a brilliant performance
Grand finale, song of the sea
Reverently performed conducted triumphantly.

Frances Gibson

Beach Dance

This now deserted shore
emptied with the approaching night.

Sunset's crimson horizon fades
beneath an amber-pink striped sky.

Along the strandline's lumpy ridge
and furrow my barefoot boys

swoop and dash.
Hunting beach glass treasure,

digging for lug worms in
quick sands at the tide's edge

where waves grow and sneak
towards those nimble hunters.

How quick they dodge backwards,
shrieking a pretence at fear.

My little silhouetted stick men
dancing as their day dies.

Pru Bankes Price

Love Is

Love is knowing that you love me.
Love is knowing that I love you.
Love is sharing our lives,
Sharing our duties,
Sharing each other.

Love is knowing each other's strength.
Love is knowing each other's failings,
Knowing each other's needs.
Love is understanding all about each other.

Love is for better or for worse.
Love is there in sickness and in health.
Love is for richer and for poorer.
Love is being together in every stage of life.

Love is being young together.
Love is enjoying each other,
In body and in mind.
Love is bearing my loved one's child.
Love is growing old together.
Love never ends.
Love endures everything.

Janet Cavill

Prince P

Prince P he's had a damn good life
Mainly because of the lady who let him make her his wife
While most people spent lots of their life working and wishing
Prince P was off hunting, shooting and fishing
During his visits abroad he often made the odd gaffe
Shrugged it off with an innocent smile a grin and a laugh
Driving carriages, taking control of the plane
There was Prince P making the news again
Walking two paces behind his wife
Yes Prince P has had a damn good life
During the forties when the world came to peace
Prince P could have gone back home to Greece
But after serving in the Royal Navy Prince P was set
To marry the young lady of high birth that he'd met
But let's give him his due, he was always here and there
Topped the engagement list nearly every year
About everything a little he seemed to know
Always willing to try things, have a go
But he's never had a mortgage, gas or electric bill
Never in the supermarket been declined at the till
I suppose with his children he's had his share of strife
But all in all Prince P has had a damn good life
Yes it was good for him when he came into our elite fold
But he's given us the DOE Awards – bronze, silver and gold
Given good support to his wife
But yes compared to most Prince P has had a damn good life.

Carl Enever

July Evening Songs Of Praise

Sunday evening Songs of Praise –
Why look there's St Mary's, Ealing –
What a beautiful church, I wonder why he
Left pulpit and calling to marry thee,
Sweet Marie the church warden's wife,
John William left his church for life.
And round the world went he, with sweet Marie.
His father, the Rev Robert of Lancs,
A Bretherton vicar was he . . .
John William trained at St Matthew's, Fulham,
For the church ministry.
(So long ago I met him,
When I was young, he tutored me)
A vicar no longer could he be,
He had to leave the ministry
Because he loved sweet Marie.
Now in Putney Vale Cemetery
In grave 336G lies JWG
And with him is his sweet Marie.
His old housekeeper, Mrs Harvey
Told us the story so long ago
(With her grandson Gordon)
She worked for him
And on his death
(Found the terrible sin) A photo –
Of Gardiner dressed for the ministry
Until he met the church warden's wife
And married sweet Marie.

Gladys Burgess

Simplicity

They say a fair exchange is no robbery
Therefore the change to humility not snobbery
Servitude not exactly the chosen norm
However a silent solace to forever warm

Memories are the reservoirs of old age
Little things are retained in happy engage
A cup of gold water given in my name
An extension of gratitude ever acclaim

Humility therefore is the essence to sustain
Simplicity in its appealing domain
Extending all of one's kindness to all
Innermost thoughts in spiralling enthrall

To be or not to be Shakespeare quotes
Within oneself a question floats
However an answer is diligently sought
To offset responses tenderly bought

Suffer not my simplicity rather compliment
Recognise the goodness a worthy stipend
No thoughts of hate indeed no trait
Suffice not to offend at any date

Hearken then to praise forthright
Virtues splendidly carried a burden light
Generously spilled out to all who receive
Blessings and happiness immediate to perceive.

Anthony McGeehan

A Wonderful Day

Oh what a wonderful day it had been
On July 22nd two thousand and thirteen
For William and Kate and their new baby boy
A day they'll remember with so much joy
Such a wonderful day for their families too
Their families in London and Buckleberry too
Looking down from Heaven was Diana it's true
So proud of Prince William, Kate, new baby too
The Queen Mother in spirit was there yes too
As she looked down from Heaven and was blessed yes too
Proud were Saint Mary's Hospital Lindo Wing
Who were involved in the birth of a future king
In Kate's village of Buckleberry there was so much joy
For Kate and Prince William and their new baby boy
For Charles, Camilla, Harry, Prince Phillip, the Queen
What a wonderful day for them all it had been
Yes how wonderful it was for us all to see
The wonderful new addition to our Royal Family
So let's not forget that special date
But remember it always and celebrate
When choosing a name you both were blessed
With George who you know will be the best
God bless you all in all that you do
God bless you all your whole life through
For a wonderful family you'll be it's true
Prince William and Kate and George yes too.

Royston Davies

How Dare The Spring?

How dare the daffodils
litter the lawns and fields and hedges
in their lovely gold profusion
and the co-op polyanthus flaunt
their gaudy oranges and purple blooms
and the birds warble and whistle
quarrelling and mating
and though tomorrow is another day
and the pink sunset evenings offer invitations
of summertime
how dare the grass grow
moss thick
and the trees sweep into blossom
into bud into leaf
as though nothing whatever has happened
how dare the spring?

I stand alone in my outrage
the long warm days
the subject of jubilation –
I stand like some misplaced harridan of doom
cursing in beds of primrose
shrieking and weeping at the wide blue sky
across which I write
don't you know – he's dead
but a high white cloud
dances across the message
and
and though nothing of import has happened
the world turns

how dare the spring?

PennyAnne Windsor

Town Garden

When springtime comes creeping in mossy-soft hose
caressing, unravelling petal and leaf;
when bluebell, convolvulus, primula, rose
take tentative glances from unwinding sheath;
when daffodils stand and defy icy-cold
Siberian snow-storms, their golden heads high
from March for St David till April when bold –
hearted George slays his dragon; then, Robin and I
venture forth once again to investigate . . .

There – stands my cherry tree:

Waiting for warmth from the sun,
She's teetering now on the edge of pale pink
while sleek starlings argue with everyone
and blackbirds shout warnings with deafening chink;
while neighbourly cats sit and wait for their chance
to pounce and destroy. Happy sparrows still chirp
from their favourite lookout, and honey bees dance
in a figure of eight, and a loving frog burps
in his pond. All's right with my world;
spring is come.

Barbara Young

Me

Born in the workhouse in 1923
It was the place I had to be
It closed down in '22
My poor dad had to get through
So he got the job straight away
Seeing his baby was on the way
Three lovely boys
He already had
And what a lovely caring dad
From the artillery he came
With his lovely name (Charley)
He loved dragging that cannon
With six white ponies
He had his fun
But he had to get that job
He had to get that couple of bob
So they gave him straight away
The tumbledown cottage, two bed
Adjoining, with no roof.
He and Maud moved in with nothing
But love and kindness
I didn't know nothing else
When I was born in '23
I was very happy
To have this lovely family around me

The boys even
Gave me their clothes
So I was a boy
Until I was eight years old
Eddy, I was called
When I went to school
Hannah More
In Trinity Road, Bristol
That was the nearest
To the workhouse
Which was down the road
16 Pennywell Road
1884, Saint Jude's, Bristol
That was it,

All the children laughed at me
And told the teacher
I was a girl
Which I was
But she said I told lies
Put me in the corner
Book above my head
I grew up looking after Ma
Who was in bed all the time
She had another baby
When I was five,
They wanted another girl like me,
Dad loved me so much
He tried and tried
Got odd jobs, doing anything

His job to keep the workhouse clean
As it went into the speaker's house,
When Lloyd George came
And the people were trying to beat him up
So he changed clothes,
With a policeman
And got out the building.

To get to the point
We had to put buckets and tin baths
In the bedroom where me and the three boys slept
In one old bed
We had bugs crawling up the walls
We had rats in every cupboard
Great big soup bowl in the kitchen
Dead people buried in the garden
Wooden crosses with only numbers,
And worse of all
We all cleaned out in the workhouse every day.

Edna Holcombe

Hair

I swung my legs backwards and forwards, like the hands of the tall clock in the hallway.
'Sit still, sweetheart,' Toby said. He pulled me back so I was sitting properly on the chair, my back against the cushion, my hair behind it. I was used to people being obsessed with my hair; girls in school assemblies used to twist bits of it around their fingers without even asking. Toby brushed it, going slowly whenever he encountered a knot, which wasn't often. I think you get knotted hair when it gets blown about by the wind. You have to go outside for that.
He started to pull strands of hair and plait them together. It was a hairstyle he'd seen on the Internet. I always asked Toby if I could go on the Internet and he would say, 'Sure sweetheart,' but then only showed me clips on Youtube.
'Have you finished yet, Toby?'
'Not yet, sweetheart.'
He tied the end of my plait with a band. I drummed my fingers against the wooden table. I was just about to get a biscuit from the tin in the corner, when I felt Toby's hand on my shoulder. He forced me back down onto the chair. He could be strong when he needed to be.
I heard the click of metal and felt my head rise up, oddly weightless. Then I felt a clump of my hair slide down my neck and saw it fall in a blonde heap around my feet.

Amy Williams

The Christmas Spirit

On Christmas Eve I walked the streets
That round a city ran
And wondered if the Christmas spirit
Had been found by Man
I looked in many faces
Questioned everyone
And searched in many places
For the spirit that was gone
Some were sober on their feet
Some lay on the ground
I then began to wonder
If it ever would be found
I visited cathedrals
And many a church pew
Sang with them their Christmas songs
Sang their carols too
They were reverent to their god
Sincerely did they sing?
But the Christmas spirit was not there
I left to find this thing
Beyond the church through falling snow
Stumbled a woman I seemed to know
She clutched a baby to her breast
Here indeed an ended quest
The woman laughed in mild surprise
But I saw God in a baby's eyes.

Robert Stevens

You Must Not Quit

No matter how rocky the road
No matter how stormy the seas
No matter if life trials
Are worse than you feel
No matter if success seems
Far out of reach
You must not quit

Life is a tiresome test
The trick is to fight it until you win
For today's troubles won't stay forever
If you have faith and belief
Just believe in yourself
Just don't quit

Life is a mission
Failure is a sum
If you get it wrong
Once, twice, thrice
Just don't quit, redo the sums
For over the horizon, is a plantation of success
With a field of riches waiting in the wings

Life is so funny, one would never have guessed
The troubles and turmoils that lie ahead
Life is a series of moments
A small measure of good times, and a great measure of bad
The trick is to treasure the good times
Store them away in your heart
And when the bad times befall you, keep smiling within
Befriend the words 'don't quit'
Find hope in all nature's gifts
For the skies in all its blueness will send a smile your way
You'll have no regrets, for you did not quit.

Karty Cole

An Olympic Vision

It is now the city of spectacle,
The serious Games begin.
At every test of sporting skill,
Of endurance and conquering will,
May the best and the bravest win.

London is the capital of the world,
A parade of every nation.
Westminster, august and solemn,
The Cenotaph and Nelson's Column,
Inspire our veneration.

The pulse of life, a mosaic of soul,
The heraldic splendour blazing,
A first vision of Big Ben
Tolling the destinies of men
Has the Olympian heart racing.

London is the centre of all things,
Of golden endeavour, the head.
Poets who dream along the Strand
With the past walk hand in hand
And converse with the holy dead.

For the past is ever present
In every regal square and arch:
The glistering dome of St Paul's
And all London's towering halls
Tell the saga of history's march.

A new day glows across the river,
On man's monumental design;
Now happy tears sting proud eyes
At every marvel and surprise
That meets with the godly skyline.

Another legend here is told
Of the Olympic flame of peace.
The gaze of the world looks upon
The tapestry of the marathon,
As once it looked on Greece.

Les Thomas

John Churchill, Duke Of Marlborough, Blenheim Palace 1704, He Never Lost A Battle

The man who never lost a battle
Stands still and silent, his eyes
Misted, is it tears of jubilation

Exultation or tears for beaten
Men upon beaten ground?
5,000 conquerors killed – 8,000 conquerors wounded.

The character of new achievements
Of men, a history of men and battles.
The man who never lost a battle
Stands still and silent.
We won, we triumph, we rejoice
The loser surrenders, succumbs and
Submits.

I am a warrior, a soldier, a man at arms
A campaigner, but still I cry
Why? What is the reason, is this
Battle for my nation, for proud
Tradition the gift of laurels to my name

The reason I cry – I cry
For men who march into battle with
Me – wise heads upon wise shoulders
Ready to bear the brunt. March into
The enemy camp, the theatre of war.

Line rank and file men, take
Orders, commands to put the flight
The enemy, push with force a
Forbidding force, gain ground, gain control.

Injuries from shot, shell
Gunpowder, bullet, bayonet mean
Wounds which maime: mutilate and
Kill, suffering severs pain.
The man who never lost a battle
Stands still and silent.

The field of battle

Yielding a stain of crimson red
The conquering air lies dormant –
Inert bodies, twisted faces, peaceful
In their long, long sleep.

Departed from this troubled
Land, regarded with honours in
The promised land.

The tired, tried and trusted
Men who survive this battle great

Sigh and seem to say, 'Thank God.
My life is safe.'

Sad and sorrowful we are for the
Men we lost on this crimson battle ground.
Proud staunch hearts, lion hearts,
We do salute all fighting men.
The man who never lost a battle
Stands still and silent.

John Churchill
Duke of Marlborough
Salutes these brave, brave men.

Christina McKechnie

No Bugles – No Drums

Discarded bayonets that once drew blood, were salvaged by quartermasters from the Flanders' mud
They knew the true value of that fine tempered steel, with its cold impersonal; – yet tactile feel
Though no weary soldier even one jot cared, that from the smelter's pot, those blades were spared
Spared for the future of wars yet to come, awaiting the clarion call, from the Bugle and the Drum
Fay politicians, complacent and supine, were deaf to those Drums, from beyond the Rhine!
Old Winston alone, knew the day would come, it was he who first heard, the Bugle and the Drum.

Battered by a Blitzkreig we stood little chance, ousted with ignominy, from battlefields of France
But young Winston at Omdurman had seen a 'Mahdi' reel, at the sight of his sabre and its cold steel!
So with commando raids, war entered a new phase, in tandem with the SAS, Europe was set ablaze
All had a preference and their quirky dislikes, but the weapon of choice was a; 'Fairburn and Sykes'
Two bespectacled gentlemen who in times of peace, served with distinction, in the 'Shanghai Police'
On the streets of that lawless city they had thrived, masters of 'ju jitzu' and fighting with knives
They trained a special cadre which stood above and apart, with every man drilled in new dark arts
Killers were created from civilian recruits, each became a warrior, instead of a mere pair of boots

They took those bayonets stained by blood, honed and shaped them and cleansed them of mud
Thus a dagger was fashioned, a true work of art and behind enemy lines it would play a deadly part
With stealth their cloak each man stayed shtum, silence replaced the Bugle and darkness the Drum
Double-edged and sleek with a needle point, balanced by a cross guard, at the bellied handle joint
Seven and half inches of fine tempered steel, perfectly weighted with an exhilarating feel
In close quarters combat, one to one, the SAS became the masters of the

much vaunted Hun
They dealt mortal wounds with a stab or a slash, or fracture a skull with a; 'Pommel Smash'
The carotid artery, or straight into the heart, were two favoured targets, on the anatomical chart
Well versed and rehearsed and mostly unseen, it became par for the course; a lethal routine!

From the Western Desert, Holland, Belgium and France, they led the enemy on a merry dance
They sheared the locks and opened the gates, stood stunned at Belsen and its wretched inmates
The guards had fled, which was just as well, for they would not have lived, their heinous tales to tell
Of honours and gongs there were scant few, certainly less, than was their hard-earned due
There were no brass hats, with enough pips and crowns, to witness deeds worthy, of stellar renown
But they created a legend which lives on today, and they did it, in their own special way
Those peerless 'originals' once of the SOE, planted the firm roots of the SAS family tree

They set the gold standard, blazed the trail and guided the regiment to its holy grail
The few that remain, are now in their tenth decade, but they've never forgotten, their stiletto blade
But they harbour no regrets, of how they used those blades; fashioned from old bayonets
Perhaps a whimsical notion, or a fain idea; – but did traces of that steel, see service in the Crimea?
Was it once in the scabbard of a brave young Hussar, on the field at Waterloo; in Boney's Abbatoir?
Is there an ephemeral spirit, through the steel passed on, to worthy successors, like a relay baton?

Destined the SAS were to inherit such a legacy, for they dashed the myth, of Germanic supremacy
With aggression, chutzpah and fox-like cunning, they rose to the challenge and made all the running
Initiative, intuition, reacting on their feet, those saboteurs and assassins became; an acclaimed elite
Beyond all doubt they were the 'real deal', the template for the 'Rangers' and

the 'Redoubtable Seals'
In any tight corner they passed every test and none could gainsay, they were; the 'best of the best'
And should all out war once again come, the SAS would do a 'curtain call', without Bugles or Drums
Many a trooper gave his life for a mate, their names are etched in stone, followed by rank and date
But forgiven they are for their mortal sins, because they lived by the maxim of 'Who Dares Wins'.

John L Horsham KC

Warm Days

Did you decide to vacate the area
As though the chap had got malaria?
When the chap uses hand lotions
You talk about heat and emotions
A chap sunbathed near the Med
A surgeon's hole was in his head
Now he has a dry handshake
And a firm grip on the garden rake.
In local parks, lovers are kissing
In summer, some gentlemen are missing.
They prefer to jog in tree-lined streets.
They use talcum powder to dry their feet.

Edward Cook

New Horizon

Leaving the past behind is done with a huff of difficulty
Years of the obvious, people, places seem rather bulky
Somewhere you called home suddenly becomes a shadow
The mind's eye makes preparations which are not too shallow
Stages emerge: looking, finding, buying and finally going
Entering a gateway of life to begin the process of sowing

Baby steps required so crawling, standing and walking
A new destination overwhelmed with trees as if stalking
Amazing how the lush colour green dominates this location
No more hustling and bustling just expect a needed vacation
The midst of the woods hisses unknown whispers blowing
Endless streams of leaves waving and clapping flowing

The winding roads cause spasms of dizziness unseen
Triumphant control over vehicles giving calm serene
The empty path draws specific attention to lonely lanes
Using the language of the countryside offering no pains
The atmospheric spirit lends itself to a time warp of still
Giving the essence of losing oneself in the name of will

A community posting inviting messages of belonging
Greetings genuine and smiles beyond facial beaming
Numerous parks equip the distribution of vast activity
Angelic sparks of stretches of grass in the open vicinity
The quietness surpasses the loudness of the old city
Pace of life acceptable and moulds without any pity

Wildlife presents itself in the scrutiny of the area of taste
Squirrels running up and down the trees with much haste
Having maximum time to fly around the birds tweet nicely
Making their presence felt and hearing a choir so brightly
Horses gallop with audiences taking intense interest
A sceneric sphere giving rise to a lifestyle of little zest

New challenges finding a platoon of understanding
Absorbing the steam of countryside so not wanting
Waves of changes blending in with the new territory
Stresses are minimised and swept away in a hurry
Abundant happiness the highlight designed in pools
A new horizon presents itself with the necessary tools.

Sonia Lahrar

Brief Deceptions

With one glance and one nod she'd be back in his arms,
Legs entwined and palms upon palms,
Just one more night – a night with no harm,
Where they both vow to create the original charm.

But moments create passions and passions lead to want,
They each slowly turn to prey – they both hunt,
They loathe that they lust but like a peacock they flaunt,
In turn they refuse but inevitably they can't.

And they're drawn in by smells, by sights, by glances,
She looks to the floor but she's not taking chances,
Her eyes peer back up and he knows they both want this,
A sheepish, shy touch; no one needs to insist,

As the sun doth arise they lay content; they awaken,
They wish to regret, a promise forsaken,
But from this elation nothing will be taken,
She turns back around and she swears now to hate him,

She looks across at him as his head ticks over,
This beautiful creature, a fallen soldier,
He pulls her towards him, he squeezes and holds her,
But he knows that this has gone too far to solder,

And briefly, they're both in a state of nirvana,
They've reached utter joy despite all the trauma,
This time could not be happier, nor calmer,
His mind fights against him; no, he does not want her,

Hard as he tries he will never replace her,
And his time later on will be dedicated to chasing her,
But he mocked and taunted and teased and defaced her,
The passions she remembered disguised what they were,

For months she suffered through days laced with pain,
And surprisingly, unwittingly, he struggled the same,
Once, her eyes lit up as she read his name,
But there had to be a time limit to this game.

When things get mistaken, deceptions created,
We rely on positives; negatives are obliterated,
We see only the happy, and not the ill-fated,
We forget the extent to which we once hated.

Alice Blackburn

Seascapes

Shades of a distant summer, the wildest waves roar
in like lions on speed or tyrannosaurus rexes preybound on shore.
Sea and sky offer visionary ranges of blues and greens,
pale onyx through azure to lapis lazuli, sapphire and ultramarine
shadows like underwater whales and basking sharks, each lazy leviathan
swimming in shifting shoals around their monumental elements,
spellbinding our hearts and heads with their massive presence
sweeping up all before them, schools of fishes and colleges of dolphins
reminding us of humanity's historic oceanic margins
after the Earth's cosmic spin-off from the aboriginal sun.

We watch the spumeous breakers crash against great granites, each one
a match for Ahab's Moby Dick, hundred foot long monsters
moving in for the kill, splattering sprays like St Valentine massacres.
As in masterworks of Newlyn School Artists, Forbes, Garstin and Harvey,
a new universe is reborn with the sights, sounds and shades of the sea.

Roland Gurney

The Village Of Aberfan

There once was a village of laughter and song
Whose people were humble, kind and strong
A place where love and affection belong
The village of Aberfan.

Just a village in Wales like so many more
Where every house kept an open door
And a welcoming smile for rich and poor
Yes this was the village of Aberfan.

And the streets of the village would ring with joy
The joy of carefree girl or boy
For life and laughter were there to enjoy
The children of Aberfan.

But the village nestled 'neath grime
A man-made mountain of coal dust and slime
And the mountain that threatened from time to time
Brought death to Aberfan.

As the little ones knelt in school to pray
Rushing and crushing it thundered their way
Just a moment in time and the children lay
Buried 'neath Aberfan.

Silent the village of Aberfan
Silent the streets where children ran
And heavy the heart and soul of Man
Who looks on Aberfan.

For the windows are shattered and prayers are said
And bells will toll as they bury the dead
And unshamed Man hangs his head
And weeps for Aberfan.

Weeps for the village so strangely still
Weeps and wonders is this thy will
Another cross on another hill
But God, why the village of Aberfan?

Let voices protest as they surely must
To the powers that be who betrayed the trust
Of our little ones let this ever be
A moment of complacency.

Noddy

Long Summer's Past

I have an old pot of sun cream in my garden shed,
I only use it when I burn so that makes it last,
We got it for the kids on holiday someplace;
And the soft scent reminds me of summers long past.

I still see it for sale on some seaside shop rack,
With the buckets and spades and crablines to cast,
But my pot is shabby and dirty and sad;
As its soft scent reminds me of summers lost past.

Some sand grains remain in the thread on the neck,
From a beach in the sun where the tide rises fast,
The kids are all grown now and leaving the nest;
But the soft scent reminds me of long summers past.

Geoff Holden

Rhymes She Didn't Learn In Nursery

Jeannie, seemly quite serene she,
How does her life progress?
With sad goodbyes, secrets and lies
She feels it's a hopeless mess.

Hey diddle diddle
She's here, in the middle,
She's jumped right over the moon.
She's smiled and she's laughed
And made such fun.
Can she please run away from this soon?

Hickory dickory dock
It's time to race the clock.
The clock says go.
She can't say no.
Hickory dickory dock.

Jeannie Jeannie sat on the fence
Couldn't come hither. Couldn't go hence.
All the reflecting from now until then
Wouldn't help Jeannie choose whether or when.

Sing a song of sixpence,
A pocketful of sighs.
Four and twenty hours
Baking porky pies.

When the pies are opened
The lies are sure to sing
And won't that be the rankish dish
To set before one's kin.

Higgledy piggledy my black heart;
It was white back at the start.
One time light, now all time dark.
Higgledy piggledy my black heart.

Round and round the problem,
Wanting to be free.
One step. Two step.
Goodbye problem. Goodbye me.

Jeanne Terry

Forward Poetry Information

We hope you have enjoyed reading this book - and that you will continue to enjoy it in the coming years.

If you like reading and creative writing drop us a line, or give us a call, and we'll send you a free information pack.

Alternatively if you would like to order further copies of this book or any of our other titles, then please give us a call or log onto our website at www.forwardpoetry.co.uk

Forward Poetry Information
Remus House
Coltsfoot Drive
Peterborough
PE2 9BF
(01733) 890099